MW01257204

Reflections from a Clay Jar

a memoir through the eyes of faith

Reverend Ingrid J. Barrett

To
My parents who gave me life
My family who gives me life
Dr. Bernard Lown who gave me the courage to live

Table of Contents

III Heart and Soul

IV Birth and Rebirth

Acknowledgements

Reflections from a Clay Jar

a memoir through the eyes of faith

Prologue

"But we have this treasure in clay jars, so that it may be
made clear that this extraordinary power belongs to God and
does not come from us."

2 Corinthians 4:7

S unshine streamed in through the studio's skylight, filling the room with
a wondrous light. Permeated with the smell of clay, the air had a dusty
feel. Potter's wheels were evenly spaced throughout the room. At one end, clay
pots, dishes, vases, and other pieces stood on the drying table, waiting to be
placed in the kiln for baking. Each piece—of fragile beauty—evoked the different
hands that had created it. Personalities unfolded in form, texture, and style.

As I entered the room, I studied the various clay creations. Mine were often
among those awaiting final firing. I collected a good amount of fresh clay and
chose a potter's wheel near the room's center. After pulling off the amount of
clay I thought I would need for a single pot, I placed it in the wheel's center. A
small pan of water stood beside me. I began kicking the foot wheel while placing
my hands over the clay. Softly and gently I moved my hands over the clay as it
spun on the wheel. As the form began to take shape, I kicked the foot wheel
harder to keep the clay moving in my hands. Adding a little water to keep the
clay soft, I started to pull up the clay. I pulled it to the desired height and then
gently pushed my fingers down into the center to begin forming my pot. I felt

my right leg working hard as my hands shaped the clay. In my bare hands the soft, moist clay felt sensuous. Through my hands I experienced the beauty of a creation unfolding. Soft and malleable now, the clay would be fragile, easily broken, when dried. It would require proper care. The wonders of clay. Wonders that live with me so many years later, wonders that inspired this book's title and scriptural text.

Both formally and informally, my ministry has taken me down many varying paths. Over the last five years one of those paths has led me to lead small group spiritual discussions on the issues that women of all ages confront today. As my groups have explored these topics, we have sought to discover how our faith and faith journeys might help us deal with these issues. Through sharing our stories, we've uncovered realizations about our faith and so have grown spiritually.

A couple of group members have suggested that I write a book. Both flattered and humbled, I dismissed the notion. Then one day this winter, I was leading a small Bible study group when I believe God stepped into the picture. Why not write a book? In the mystery of that moment, I felt God's call to write about my spiritual journey. All that day I reflected on the many events in my life that I now could see were very spiritual. An outline took shape in my mind, and the Scripture from 2 Corinthians played over and over in my heart. Why not start and see where it leads? And so, this spiritual journey began.

My life began to stretch before me in my writing. I reflected again and again that life is mine to live, and that I have been blessed with the treasure of the light of the gospel of Jesus Christ. But this extraordinary power is not of me but of God, because I'm but a fragile clay jar molded by the hand of God. By opening my eyes and my heart to God, I have discovered more fully this treasure. As I put my life's stories into words, my being is open to and empowered by God's working in my life. With each story I reflect that I am but a clay jar and that the true power of my life and ministry are of God. And thus, these stories are reflections from a clay jar.

I have written this book not only for my family and friends but for all who wonder where God is in their lives. For all who wonder about their spiritual journey. For all who, through the stories of my life, might see God working in their own lives. With prayer and reflection, I have discovered that my life has indeed been full of spiritual encounters and the message of God's loving presence. My hope is that those who read this book might, upon reflection, come to know God's presence through their own stories. Come to know, not *about* God, but to know God Himself moving in and through their lives. Come to know that they, too, are on spiritual journeys, journeys that are rich and full because none of us walks the path alone, but we all walk it in the presence of the Holy One.

Land and Water

ONE

The Garden

"For God is love."
1 John 4:8

September found me in the main schoolhouse building, which seemed enormous to me because I was only six years old. Off the second-story hall, there were four doors to classrooms for four different grades. My new classroom was at the opposite end of the hall from the stairs that led up the front of the building. It was the one on the left just before you turned the corner to the hallway leading to the rest of the building. To be in first grade up here on the second floor felt momentous. Like many firsts, my introduction to my classroom was a bit scary. The desks were lined up neatly in four rows facing the blackboard and the teacher's desk. As I entered, I wondered where I should sit. Was it better to sit in the front row or to be safely inconspicuous in the back? Only time would tell.

First grade would bring many new experiences, so the year stretched before me like a meadow promising to burst into bloom. Among many other events, I looked forward to the flower show that the class would host in the spring. These many years later, some of the show's details have faded. But every time I see grass being grown in eggshells at Easter, I vividly recall the time and effort that the students put into their exhibits. Once more I see our classroom, where twenty-some egg cartons held eggshells that had grass growing in varying stages. Tall grass needing a haircut, tiny bits of grass barely peeking from the soil. No matter how well we did or did not succeed in growing grass, our teacher encouraged us to bring our cartons in for the show. It was spring, the season of rebirth and growth. We were to witness this growth in the green grass, with help from the sun's light and warmth, and the care we provided.

Now, as those eggshells fill my memory, I better understand the lesson to be learned. I wonder if that's the point of much of our early learning: the images we store away, images that take on greater meaning as we age. Such is the case with my spiritual journey. As my faith has grown over fifty-odd years, springtime has become more and more powerful for me. Our good earth lies dormant for months, bearing seeds and plants that wait for the soil to warm and thereby signal that now it is time to grow. Growth. Life. Lessons that themselves lay dormant and grew within me. Creation a wonder. Grass turning brilliant green after the snow has melted touches me now. There wells up within me a sense of renewal and rebirth. Simple blades of grass grow together to create a soft green carpet of joy, deep as their roots.

When I look around at nature, it appears busy and complex, but that's only the impression from a passing glance. I learned a different lesson from the flower show. Flowers and grasses—nature—have wondrous simplicity as well.

The center of the flower show was the dish gardens, which had to fit on each student's desk and have living plants. The garden would be displayed all day, so our desks would become gardens. We students had to make many decisions. Where to start? With a theme? A dish? We had to imagine and then create what we imagined. For weeks before the show, we discussed the gardens we might create. Many of my friends had elaborate plans that I found intimidating. In contrast, I focused on a simple theme. I began to gather what I would need.

Even my smaller toys were too big for my miniature garden. Then I came across two ceramic figurines of perfect size: Lady and Tramp from the Disney motion picture. Now to create the scene. All I wanted was a simple garden. My mother and I found a green ceramic bowl just the right size for my desk. Outside I wandered in search of plant material and came across a Japanese maple in our side yard. The branches hung gracefully toward the ground. I cut off a small branch. Perfect. There was the tree for my garden. Moss grew beneath the tree. There was the grass for my garden. Perfect.

Now to put it all together. I filled the bowl with dirt, placed moss on top, and stuck the single branch into the dirt. I then placed Lady and Tramp under the weeping branch. I knew the two Disney characters loved each other and so went back outside and picked a small white blossom from one of my mother's plants. With a tiny piece of tape, I attached the blossom to Tramp's mouth. Done. The scene seemed magical. In the shade of a tree, Tramp offered Lady a flower as a token of his love. I worried, though. Was it too simple? What would others think? Did it look as if I hadn't put enough time and effort into the project? But then, as now, the garden evoked good emotions.

One more task: every garden had to have a name. Love was center stage in the garden. "Lady's in Love," I proudly wrote on a three-by-five card in my best handwriting. Everything was ready to go.

When I brought my garden to school the next day, I looked around and saw the elaborate gardens my friends had created. There were farms and forests, numerous plastic figurines, gravel, rocks, and fences made out of Popsicle sticks. My heart sank, but I still hoped to win a ribbon. So I placed my garden on my desk, sat, and waited to see what would happen.

By grades, the rest of the school came to visit the first grade flower show. My teacher, Mrs. Wigan, asked the students to stand by the desk of their favorite dish garden. Class after class, most of the students stood by my desk. That's when the excitement for me began. When the kindergartners came, more than half of them stood around me. They were only a year younger, but I felt like a big person that day. As they huddled around my desk, I was almost smothered by them. They loved *my* garden, not the busy gardens with all the figures and plants. They knew the story of *Lady and the Tramp*. My simple garden must have revived emotions they had felt while watching the movie.

My dish garden won the blue ribbon, but the power of the day and the garden have continued to grow within me. "Lady's in Love" has taken on new meaning. Yes, there remains the satisfaction of a job creatively done. But now I also see what others must have seen that day.

Our lives are so full, so busy. Our lives are filled with so much stuff. I think we like to tell ourselves we enjoy the busyness or, better yet, we need all that stuff for some reason. One of my friends crammed as many buildings, fences, plants, people, and animals as he could into his garden.

Far too many of us live in such gardens. It was fun to look at, but oozed a feeling of chaos.

Creation can present itself complex and massive. But each thing created by God is also intricate, made up of a thousand simple elements. Pausing to look at the simple pieces brings new meaning. A branch, some moss, two figures, and a single white bud in a lover's mouth. Those who loved my garden saw the beauty of this simplicity, especially the simplicity of life that radiates love.

Since I created my garden, I—like other adults—have encountered many complex life situations. As life becomes more "serious" with age, it's easy to lose childlike simplicity. Instead of seeing life through the wide eyes of a child, we analyze and calculate. So it has been with my spiritual windings. I found myself getting entangled in the many complexities that make up faith. Like different dish gardens, many worldviews compete for our understanding of life. Faith is one of them. How complex does a faith need to be? Should it, instead, be simple?

As I have struggled with my faith, my heart keeps coming back to the simple. Back to what I can truly digest. Back to what stems from the heart and soul. Doctrine grounds my faith, but at some point I need to put aside the many words of doctrine and religion and return to the heart to find God's uncomplicated love, the same love depicted in my dish garden. God doesn't expect us to understand it all. Rather, God seeks a relationship. God always extends the white flower of love, "for God is love" (1 John 4:8). As my faith journey has matured, the faith that God loves all of us unconditionally and each of us personally has only increased. Toward God and others, our hearts should be like those of first graders. God offers us love. This is a simple offering, as simple as a single white bud blooming after a long, dark winter. Do we have the faith to smile and embrace this offering? To trust God enough to accept it?

"God is Love." That should be the title of our earthly dish garden. A simple faith in God speaks from the heart and has the power to move us through life's complexities. Like grasses, trees, and flowers in spring, faith is reborn and grows in a simple way.

TWO

Sailing

"The wind blows where it chooses."
John 3:8

Growing up near a river and the ocean, I learned to sail at the early age of eight. My father and older brother were avid sailors, so I wanted to learn to sail as well. The first boats we sailed were single-sail Turnabouts that one or two people could handle. During the first couple of summers of sailing classes, we all had the opportunity to alternately be skipper and crew, learning the skills of each. The skills came easily to me; I possessed a certain knack for a sailboat. From the beginning, I loved to sail and be out on the river.

Our sailing instructor taught us how to race. We learned how to maneuver upwind and downwind, how to start, and the rules of sailboat racing. I can still recall some of the "discussions" we had after a race as to who had had the right of way or who could be disqualified for not following the rules. Within three years I graduated from Turnabouts to a Blue Jay sailboat, which had a mainsail and a jib and required one crew member for racing.

I reflect on the summer I sailed a Blue Jay, which was painted a purplish color. My yacht club held races every Saturday and Sunday. Every weekend afternoon I found a crew and set out for the boathouse. The Blue Jays were kept out of the water and so needed to be launched every time they were taken out. Learning to launch a boat is not hard but does take some practice. Once safely in the water, the boat is rigged and readied for the race. The commodore set the course, and the time came for us to be out on the river headed for the starting line.

Coming from its usual afternoon direction out of the southeast, the wind was gentle as I headed out of the boat basin. The first mark usually was Pleasure Bay buoy, down and across the river. As we rounded the dock, steadier wind filled the sails, and the boat picked up speed. The wind was perfect for sailing, brisk but not overwhelming and not a fluky land breeze. I felt comfortable behind the helm and sailed around the starting line in preparation for the start. The minutes on my stopwatch clicked down to the last seconds. I came downwind to the windward starting mark with perfect timing. Just as the starting gun went off, I pulled up into a hard starboard tack at the mark. Because my boat was windward to the rest of the fleet, I had clear wind. My boat began to pull away from the others on the first tack. When all the boats made their first tack I could see I was in the lead. I rounded the first mark in first place. "Great way to begin!" I whispered to myself.

As we sailed on a leech to the second mark, my Blue Jay opened a gap. My lead had increased by the time we rounded the second mark and headed downwind. As we rounded the mark, our spinnaker went up flawlessly. Setting the spinnaker seemed so easy on this day, but many times my spinnaker had come out of its bag upside down. That was always disastrous. Two or three boats could pass you while you reset the spinnaker and got it filled with wind. A blessing when the maneuver went well, a curse when it did not. It was all in the packing of the spinnaker in its bag. The top had to be carefully identified and loaded in last so it was the first thing seen as you prepare to round the mark and the first thing up the forestay on the spinnaker halyard.

The wind filled the balloon-like sail, and my boat flew with the wind. This leg of the race required little work other than to keep the boat on the right course and occasionally trim the spinnaker. Whereas I felt the wind in my face when tacking to the first mark, the wind was gentle yet powerful downwind as it blew at my back and filled the big sail. I ran the rest of the course fast that day and won the race.

In learning to race, I learned how to manage the boat and its riggings and acquired knowledge of the wind. The better I could read the wind, the better I could race. Watching the wind come across the river and reading its direction was paramount. I learned to pick out a puff and handle a lull. I watched the sail, which told me if I was reading the wind correctly. I began to enjoy the hard blows and soft land breezes. Each required its own art in racing. I learned to appreciate and respect the wind. Many an afternoon the wind had a mind of its own, and I was at its mercy.

My Blue Jay turned out to be a fast boat. No matter how well they're sailed, some boats simply are not as fast as others. My boat moved well and seemed to skim effortlessly over the water. As the summer progressed, I rose to the top spot within my sailboat class. I felt incredibly gratified. By the end of the season, I had earned the right to go to the Blue Jay national sailing regatta on Long Island Sound in New York. I was thrilled but somewhat scared. This racing would be a whole different type of sailing. I would be matched against the best from all over the country on a body of water very different from my river. Most likely the wind would be much stronger, and there would be waves and swells.

Towing my boat, I drove to Long Island with my crewmate Charlotte. All boats had to conform to precise dimensions. Terrified and overwhelmed, I waited in line as sails were measured. Some were fine; others needed to be altered. My main and jib met the specifications, but my spinnaker was too large. It had to be cut down. I had assumed since I had a new boat, its sails would be fine. Cutting them to precise dimensions proved to be daunting. Dealing with the same problem, the man just ahead of me knew of a place, near the marina, to get sails recut. He kindly gave me directions. I arrived and entrusted my spinnaker to the sail cutter's hands. He chopped off my sail. I returned to the sailing committee and was relieved to find that the sail cutter had done the job correctly. My sails passed, and I was ready to go—the first of many hurdles to be jumped that weekend.

The next hurdle came during the first race. The wind shrieked across the Sound. Some boats overturned and ended up floating in the whitecapped waves. It became a day of *can I keep my boat upright, and me and my crew out of the drink?* I especially remember one downwind leg. The wind pulled our spinnaker so hard that I thought our bow would go under as it cut through the waves. My crew and I hiked out from the stern, desperately trying to add enough weight in the back to keep the boat on an even keel. The wind threatened to rip the boat apart and tossed it around like a toy. I was frightened. I gained a huge amount of respect for the wind that afternoon.

We came in last, but to our credit, we finished the race. Many boats had to be towed to shore and many sailors fished out of the water. My crew and I were sopping wet from the spray of the boat cutting through the waves. The experience had been alternately terrifying and exhilarating. All afternoon I saw the wind's effects on the water and sailors.

Wind is not visible to the eye. We know it's there by what we feel and what we see. In this, it makes its power known. To be able to read the wind is imperative, a learned and practiced skill from many days on the water.

Another vivid recollection is of days sailing when there was far too little wind or none at all. In some ways this is more difficult than experiencing too much wind. Often, lacking wind, I would thrash the boat around, trying to get it to move in the water. Usually I just knocked the wind out of the sails which often caused the boat to sail backward. The frustration of it all. I soon discovered the art of sailing a boat in an extremely light wind.

During summer regattas, my sailing club competed against other boat clubs. The club hosting a particular invitational would designate the type of boats to be sailed. One particular regatta was to be sailed in Sailfish. Having never sailed a Sailfish, I was thrilled. At my age, the possibility of flipping the boat over and being forced into the water was exciting. This was going to be fun regardless of how well our club did.

Dressed in our bathing suits, we were assigned boats and headed out to the starting line. A Sailfish can be sailed by one person, but we set out two to a boat because we were young and small. As the afternoon began, there was scant wind. I was somewhat disappointed that the boat would not tip over. It was hot. I had looked forward to a dip in the river and the need to right the boat. When I think back on my many sailings in a Sailfish, I realize that it was tipping over that made them so much fun. Often we flipped on purpose, to enjoy a swim.

This day the races were being held on a different river than I usually sailed on. The wind patterns were very different here, so our club was badly beaten in the first race. Unlike the members of my club, the sailors from the hosting club knew where they would encounter wind or calm. By the end of the morning, I was becoming familiar with the wind patterns, so I did better in the race just before lunch. After lunch the sailors headed out for the day's final races. Instead of picking up, as it usually did in the afternoon, the wind continued to die down. The racing became very slow and frustrating. The sailboats drifted during so much of the first race that the race committee considered canceling the last race because the wind was getting so light. But the race proceeded.

That last race was painful. All the boats drifted across the starting line. On the way to the first mark, we watched the water very carefully so that we could catch that breeze and make some progress. From there we drifted into the next breeze. The water was like glass on some parts of the river. I tried to avoid spots that I could see lacked wind. We took advantage of any puff. When I reached the last mark, I rounded it in nearly last place. The last leg was downwind to the finish line. All the boats slowed to almost a complete stop.

At this point the wind had all but died. The last leg was so tedious and boring that some kids jumped off their boats and swam around. No one physically pushed their boat, but that was a very tempting strategy. Some yelled back and forth among the boats. Would we, could we, actually finish the race?

Far back in the fleet, I simply sat. No way could I win. As I sat contemplating my fate, suddenly my boat slightly picked up speed. I was catching the slightest breeze. I told my crew not to move so that we wouldn't rock the boat at all. We sat very still. Our boat continued to move through the calm water. We passed the boat in front of us and then the next boat. We inched up on the next one. We remained motionless, like wooden figures pasted on top of a Sailfish. It seemed magical that our stillness caused our boat to move. We didn't even talk. I sat with my hand lightly resting on the tiller. About halfway down the final leg, I needed to make a minor correction in direction. Otherwise, we remained motionless. The stiller we sat, the faster the boat moved, because we kept from disturbing any wind that might hit our sail. The kids from the other boats started to shout at us. "What are you doing? Got your motor on?" We sailed past all the other boats and won the race. We had preserved a fragile wind and, through our stillness, allowed it to move us forward. In surrendering to the wind, the boat moved forward. The touch of breeze that we were able catch was ultimately the master of the race.

While sailing, I learned a lot about the wind. I came to recognize the uniqueness of it in each sail. I learned how to use the wind and how to let the wind propel my boat. I gained respect for its power, whether in force or in gentleness. Through these experiences, I understand now the many and varied characteristics of the wind—its dynamics and its life force. It has become a very spiritual presence for me, because, through it, I embrace and better understand the Holy Spirit.

The gift of the Holy Spirit is like the wind. It first comes upon Jesus' disciples with a rush:

> When the day of Pentecost had come, they were all together in one place. And suddenly from heaven there came a sound like the rush of a violent wind, and it filled the entire house where they were sitting . . . All of them were filled with the Holy Sprit. (Acts 2:1–2, 4)

If I close my eyes and ponder this biblical event, I feel wind hitting me. It moves across my face and reaches into my heart. For me the description of the coming of the Holy Spirit at Pentecost is powerful. If you know the wind as I know it from sailing, this event takes on its own life, its own meaning. Just as the wind hit my sails, the Spirit comes upon me and all of us.

As in sailing, wind is unpredictable. "The wind blows where it chooses, and you hear the sound of it, but you do not know where it comes from or where it goes. So it is with everyone who is born of the Spirit" (John 3:8). I have felt the Spirit move among us in unpredictable ways. I have felt its guidance in the power or gentleness of the moment. Like the wind, it sometimes comes from unknown places. I feel it in the air, surrounding and holding me. I find holiness in its unpredictability. It is of God, not of this world. It touches me at God's will, not mine, and brings me to wonderment. As the wind moves in my life, so does the Holy Spirit.

Jesus promised us, "If you love me, you will keep my commandments. And I will ask the Father, and he will give you another Advocate, to be with you forever. This is the Spirit of truth . . . You know him, because he abides with you and he will be in you" (John 14:15–17). I believe in this life-giving gift. As the wind moves in my life so, too, does the Holy Spirit. As the wind comes from different directions with varying strength so, too, does the Holy Spirit. There have been times when the presence of the Spirit is so strong it has almost knocked me over.

I reflect on one of the more powerful times in my most recent past. After five years as the sole pastor of a small church, I was pleased with how my ministry had unfolded there. The congregation and I had built a stronger Christian community. And then this restless feeling began to creep in ever so slightly. As I read the writings of church consultants regarding the direction churches should be moving in the twenty-first century, I found myself intrigued with this new church model. Intrigued, I read still more. I also attended conferences and workshops on emerging ideas and ministries. I felt the Spirit guiding me toward a new ministry. The Spirit took on a life of his own. I found myself no longer crawling toward a new ministry but running toward one.

Like the wind on Long Island Sound, the Spirit was blowing on me and within me. I was called to move on, to work directly with people, especially those who had no church home, hadn't attended church, or had a negative reaction to the traditional church. I strongly believe that the Holy Spirit called me to those who were spiritually hungry and previously unable to find and know God. The Spirit told me that the church is not a building; the church is the people: "Go find those people, no matter how few or many. Let the wind fill your heart." I left the traditional church and after a year of study, prayer, and conversation began a ministry of small groups who meet in my home. We reflect on how the Scriptures might help us deal with life's issues. Guided by the Spirit, we can walk a faith journey and be transformed.

Just as the Spirit blew with great force leading me into a radical ministry, there have been times in which it is only as I sit very still that I sense God, through the Spirit, touching my life in a quieter, more mysterious way. An incident comes to mind. In many ways it was like the day on the Sailfish when I did not try to control the wind but let it be and let it do.

One day, I knew something was wrong as soon as my daughter walked into the kitchen after school. Her face and voice conveyed devastation. Her life was "over," she declared. Feeling helpless and inadequate, I sat and listened. What could I possibly do? My motherhood was in serious danger of falling flat on its face. Ultimately, I could say nothing and, therefore, did nothing. My daughter went off to her room torn to pieces, and I was left standing in the kitchen by myself.

Then a presence led me up to my bedroom. I believe it was the gentleness of the Holy Spirit guiding me to the solace of a private corner. I slid to my knees and began to pray. I found it in my heart to pray softly and calmly. I laid before the Lord all my fears, feelings of inadequacy, and frustration. I let it flow out of me until I felt empty. In that stillness I listened. I placed myself in the hands of the Spirit and the mercy of his blessings. I knelt for quite a while. As I recall, there was no great epiphany, just a feeling of calm. The restlessness of the heart had been replaced with the gentleness of the Spirit giving me strength to go back to my daughter and be a loving mother as best as I was able. Perhaps I didn't need to do anything for her. I needed to be a presence of comfort and love by just being there.

I needed to place my heart in the hands of the Holy Spirit and allow his gentle breezes to lead me. As I have stopped trying to *know about* the Holy Spirit, but come to *know* the Holy Spirit, I feel him abiding with me, and I find myself believing that the Spirit is in me as he is in others. Like in sailing, the wind became a part of me and the boat in which I was sailing; so as I invite the Spirit to abide in my life, I feel his presence along my faith journey. In the sailing races of life the Holy Spirit is there to comfort, strengthen, and guide. I have faith in that. I believe that as surely as the wind wafts across my cheeks.

THREE

The Tower

"Choose this day whom you will serve."
Joshua 24:15

My good friend Marcy presented me with the keys in the back hallway of our high school dormitory. She pulled a long chain from her pocket. More than a dozen keys dangled from it. As she moved the chain in front of my eyes, the keys rattled invitingly. They were mine now. There was no pomp and circumstance, just an entrusting of the keys from one to another. I took the keys into my hand, held them up, and felt their notable weight. The keys had seen many owners and had been passed down through the years. Why I had been chosen to be their next owner was not clear at this ceremony—a quiet ceremony with just the two of us hidden away from others in the building.

Which door each key unlocked was not known. But three keys were clearly marked. They unlocked the doors to the tower. At each floor leading up to the tower, a locked door barred access to the next level. My friend described the ascent to each level and what I might find there. I tried to picture the rooms. Tucking the keys into my book bag, I thanked her for this awesome gift. I felt pride and a sense of responsibility. When I graduated, I would choose the next recipient of "the keys." Over the years rumors about the keys had floated around the school, but no one seemed to know much about them other than that they unlocked places off-limits to students. In my bag, they represented forbidden possibilities waiting to be unlocked.

For many days I wondered if I should defy the rules and use the keys. Life is easier if you follow the rules. Unlike others in my class, I had learned quickly what was expected. I wasn't one to challenge the establishment, but it was perhaps "the" thing to do when I was in high school. I don't believe it's a whole lot different in today's world than it was then in the '60s. However, the risks are greater in today's world. But I believe it is within the hormones of a teenager to push buttons and push some more to see what one can get away with.

Choice is a gift, a gift from God. God wants us to make wise choices. It is up to us to decide which choices are wise and which are not. The keys gave me new choices. With them I could go places I had never been before—mysterious, forbidden places. Places where I might not even have dared to go because to do so would be to bend the rules just a mite too far. But maybe it is in the taboo factor that temptation lies. To be instructed to avoid a thing represents a temptation for us "rebellion-prone" creatures. Coupled with a passion for a thing I loved, I would eventually venture forth. Would it be a good choice? Only time would tell. Was it a wise choice? Probably not, because of the potential consequences. Choice and consequence make quite the pair. You have wrestled with them; I have wrestled with them. Who has a history of wisdom, of victory?

The end of the school year approached and with it the final athletic competitions. Our school was divided into two teams—green and purple—that competed throughout the year in different sports, accumulating points. As a member of the green team, I had acquired quite an assemblage of green things, including a green hand-knit sweater stretched two sizes too large for me by my senior year, and a bike, built from an array of parts, painted green. Uniquely ugly, my bike was the most popular on campus. Funny how that is.

The final field day was just days away. Something had to be done to psyche out the purple team and assert green supremacy. My athleticism certainly would help my team, but I wanted to do something more. In my book bag, the keys rattled a daring answer.

In my fervor to make a statement for our team, I made the choice of going ahead with a plan I had been scheming. The weekend before the big games, I went to the local department store and bought green crepe paper, heavy tape, and wire. A couple of nights passed without my daring to follow through. Would I have the nerve? Then came the night, calm and moonlit. The gray gothic buildings cast jagged shadows on the lawns. When the dorm lights finally went out and most of the students descended into sleep, I lay awake in my bed not moving a muscle, pretending to sleep. The clock ticked its way to two a.m. I slipped a sweatshirt over my pajamas, gathered my supplies, and took "the keys." As quietly as possible, I crept out of my room and into the hall toward the stairs. And so it began.

There was enough light in the halls for me to move easily toward the first door to be unlocked. I slipped behind the storage closet in one corner of the dorm. There it was. With trepidation I put the first key into the lock and wondered if it would, in fact, unlock the door. The key in the lock made a sound that I thought would wake the dead. Of course that was just my imagination—I was sure someone was going to pop out of the shadow and catch me red-handed. I quietly pushed the door and found myself on the other side before I could comprehend what I'd just done.

Entering a musty room, I closed the door behind me. Old pieces of furniture were piled here and there. The room reeked of the past. I pulled my flashlight from my pocket and cast its light around the room to get my bearings. I soon turned it off, because I didn't want someone to see the light and come investigate. I walked around the furniture until I reached ladderlike wooden stairs leading to the next level. The room contained just enough moonlight for me to climb the stairs to the ceiling. At the top, I stopped, poked my head up through the hole, and surveyed the room I was about to enter. I didn't want any surprises.

I stepped up into the room and again turned on my flashlight. Its light revealed wooden beams, supports, and much dust. In the middle of the room was another ladderlike wooden staircase, unfinished and not very worn. I climbed the ladder to the top and confronted a locked trapdoor. Out came the keys. Being on the ladder, I fumbled with them, looking for the right one. I tried two that didn't work. The third went into the lock, and I carefully opened it. With some effort, I pushed the trapdoor to one side. Once more I poked my head up to survey the next level. It, too, was empty except for exposed beams and supports.

As I pulled myself onto my feet, I felt a draft—cold night air floating through wood and stones. I was in the tower, headed to the highest spot on campus. Was I cold from the night air or from fear at my own boldness? I contemplated quitting but decided I had come too far to go back. The keys had proven reliable. They had helped me reach my first goal.

Marcy had told me that the wooden ladder now in front of me provided the final ascent to the top of the open tower. The ladder felt flimsy as I made my way to the top. Once again there was a locked trapdoor over my head. I found the third key. It turned the lock and released the door. I placed the keys in a pocket of my pajamas to ensure that I wouldn't lose them during my descent. As I poked my head up through the trapdoor, a rush of cold air hit my face. I paused and looked around. The night sky was before me. Lights from the campus and town appeared below. Suddenly, a pigeon fluttered over my head. Then a second and third. I wondered if I had frightened them as much as they had startled me. Especially because I'm afraid of heights, I thought, "What am I doing up here?"

Fear is a curious thing. It takes on many faces in varying circumstances and can morph into sheer horror in a split second. What form would it take this night? As I pulled myself to my feet and looked out, I froze with fear at the tower's great height. The tower stood majestically above the campus, a landmark for the city surrounding it. Looking up at it from the campus grounds it looked tall, but standing up there with the night wind blowing in my face, I felt as if I was atop the earth. The night wind blew in my face. There were no walls, only stone supports about ten feet high holding up the crown. The floor, of blue stone, felt uneven under my feet. I froze for a moment to get my bearings and regain my nerve. Would fear keep me from ultimately accomplishing my mission? I was inches from my goal. I moved carefully toward the stone support facing the campus's inner quad. I worked quickly but very carefully. When I was done, I glanced out on the campus once more before I slowly backed up to the trapdoor. As I went down the ladder, my heart stopped pounding quite so hard. Mission accomplished.

I easily retraced my steps. As I left each room, I locked each door behind me with one of the sacred keys. I soon was back in bed. I lay shaking from the cold, wondering if I would be caught and disciplined for my actions. But who would know? Who would know it was me in the tower?

The next morning dawned clear—a sunny spring day. I couldn't wait to get to the quad and view my handiwork. Others had arrived there long before me. People talked and pointed as they looked up at the esteemed school tower. There, flying from the tower, were green crepe streamers. They floated in the wind above the whole campus. Green was on top, at the height of its glory. Everyone wondered who had done the deed. I didn't say anything to anyone, just watched those green streamers flying high and handled the keys in my pocket.

What are we willing to risk and for what purpose? As I reflect on that night and day, I see myself having the courage to take risks for the passion of the moment. Was my action wise? Probably not. When I think now about the potential consequences, I shudder. Still, in my mind's eye, those streamers continue to float in the wind of risk and rebellion. The memory is vivid and calls me to reflect on the choices of the present.

Do risk and rebellion join hands to our peril, or do they simply testify to our desire for challenge, our desire for change? Are these forces spurred from the outside world or do they grow from the inner self? Perhaps one piggybacks on the other. Surely there are places we should not have gone, for any number of reasons. There are also situations that have provided an insurmountable challenge. There are situations in which you knew deep within that something needed to change. Does the glory of the risk drive you down those roads? Or is it something more—a reckless spirit of rebellion? This gift of choice is not always an easy gift to manage. Much that is happening in today's world seems to motivate rebellion in some form, or it teases us with a desire for risk. The choice is ours. The question is how to use those choices for the benefit of not just the "green team," but for the society in which we live.

Where is risk, where is rebellion leading us today? Are there streamers of green crepe paper flying in the wind? Do we silently own them? Do we admire them from a distance? Are we willing to take risks that reflect our personal convictions? Do we join the team of wise risk-takers? Or do we walk away in fear and apathy? The choice is ours.

FOUR

Rowing

"A time for every matter under heaven"
Ecclesiastes 3:1

Dawn broke with glorious yellows and oranges splashed against a pale blue sky. The sky was cloudless, and the trees became silhouetted against the colors of the morning. The lake was calm, and the daylight slowly made the water sparkle. I sat in the middle of the lake in my rowing shell, mesmerized by the morning's beauty. It had been pitch black when I had launched my shell. Over many mornings I had grown accustomed to beginning my rowing practices in the dark. We had to start by five a.m. to get in a full workout and be back at the college in time for eight a.m. classes. Dragging ourselves out of bed so early seemed way beyond the call of duty, but if we wanted to row every day and have time for everything else in our lives, five a.m. practices were necessary. The darkness always seemed to overwhelm, but the promise of sunrise made the effort worthwhile.

With light on the water now, we could pick up the pace of the practice. The hour before had been spent in warm-ups and drills. Back and forth, up and down the lake we rowed with our coach barking at us through his bullhorn. Usually, two or three shells were on the water at each practice. We would row in time with each other, then split off to practice starts or other techniques on our own. Being in a single scull, I found it somewhat difficult to maneuver in the darkness, but each time I managed to stay in sync with the practice schedule. After there was enough light on the water for me to clearly see where I was going, my coach would put me through my paces. He scrutinized every stroke. Were my hands properly aligned? Were my oars in the water at the optimal depth for speed? Were they barely skimming across the top of the water on the recovery stroke?

Often I felt like a well-greased machine. In and out, in and out, back and forth, back and forth on the shell's sliding seat. When I had the rhythm right, I seemed to fly across the water. Each stroke felt effortless. However, on many mornings I simply couldn't get it right.

Trying so hard to keep my hands close together as they crossed over on the recovery part of the stroke, I found my knuckles bleeding by the end of practice. My knuckles took such a beating, my mother worried that they would be scarred for life. Forty years later I look down at them and see only the slightest trace of some scars, some unevenness of skin. Over the years the skin has healed remarkably well. Only I can see the memories etched in my right hand.

The coolness of early morning felt good at the end of the workout. My shirt was damp from perspiration and an occasional splashing from the oars. After washing down the shells and storing our equipment, we rowers headed out for a four-mile run, the distance around the lake. Many times I wondered if my tired legs could carry me all the way around. Although motley-looking, we ran as a team, encouraging one another to keep going and working for a common goal. In June came the Nationals, and that was where we were headed. We worked hard, because we wanted to compete well and possibly win a few races. So we ran on tired legs around the lake before getting back into our cars and returning to campus.

By my fourth year of rowing, I came to love our early morning practices and the glorious sunrises. Even now, so many years later, when I witness a sunrise, I recall the lake, its stillness, and the brilliant colors bouncing off of it. Good memories. Interesting how little things can spark in our minds and hearts vivid memories of the past. What a gift that can be, most particularly when the joy of the moment is brought to the surface. I believe sometimes we let the failures, the bad times, dominate those memories. These occasions creep so easily to the forefront. One negative experience can outweigh ten joyous ones if we allow it. I could think of the ache in my legs, the soreness of my shoulders, my pounding heart, my bloody knuckles—or I could hold close the colors of the morning, the friends and teammates, and the rhythm of oars. I have chosen over the years to keep the latter close to my heart.

My rowing career blossomed over a three-year span. I rowed in every type of shell: eights, quads, pairs, and singles. Ultimately, rowing a single shell became my passion. At this time in the history of women's rowing in the United States, there were few women's teams. Most were at West Coast schools, so I was fortunate to attend a California college. Otherwise I might not have rowed. Back then, rowing shells were made primarily for men, which meant the shells were heavy. My senior year I was offered an opportunity I could not pass up. A premier shell manufacturer offered to make a woman's single shell just for me. It would be lighter than the standard shell. My parents' generosity enabled me to have the shell made. Today I reflect back and give thanks that my parents understood and felt my passion for rowing. There was one hitch. My father insisted that I sell the shell after graduation, because he didn't think rowing should be one of my lifetime sports, because it was less than ladylike. But that was okay; I could pursue my dream for a year.

My new shell was beautiful and so light that I could easily place it in the water and lift it out by myself. The oars came unpainted, so I lovingly painted them two shades of blue. A year of hard training began. I pushed hard when I rowed by myself in practice, rowed against other shells, or rowed in fall meets. The clock became my enemy and my friend. Every minute was important. As the fall rowing season approached an end, my times decreased. As the winter season neared its end, I knocked even more minutes off my time. By spring season I was down to shaving seconds off my best times. Every second mattered. Why every second? Rowing races come down to minutes or seconds. I was concentrating on the 500-meter dash. In this short race there was not a second, or fraction of a second, to be wasted.

Practicing my starts became paramount. The faster I could get off the starting block, the better my position for the rest of the dash. A second lost at the start would be very difficult to make up. As the California winter air began to warm, I could feel my muscles move more easily and quickly in rowing workouts. It took less time to warm up, so there was more time during practices to work hard. I would start again and again. My coach would note every detail that could be improved. I felt frustration. "I can't do this any better," I thought. "I can't do this any faster." But my coach believed in me, and he had a contagious passion for rowing. We could do this together.

June arrived and with it the Nationals. I would row in races with my teammates, but the 500-meter was for me alone to win, if I could put all those practice hours together one last time. The day of the race finally dawned. I was not on the lake early that morning, but fantasized about how beautiful it must have been. I was in my apartment trying to stay calm and remember everything I had learned over the last four years.

When we rowers got to the lake, it was like glass. I felt relief: without wind, rowing a record time was within reach. The sun would be hot, but the race was short, so heat shouldn't be a factor. The Nationals were being held on our lake this year, so I had the "home field" advantage. I wouldn't have to travel. I wouldn't have to row on an unfamiliar lake.

As the women's rowing teams assembled, there was a sense of ordered chaos. All those women getting organized and ready, yet knowing exactly what needed to be done and when. Like the other rowers, I carefully checked my equipment. Everything was in order, and I was ready to go when my race was called.

I don't remember the exact time that the race began. It was sometime in the morning in the middle of the regatta. As I pushed off from the dock, I breathed a sigh of relief, because all the training and all the waiting were finally over. The race loomed very close. I launched with plenty of time to make my way to the starting line. My shell floated gently over the water as I warmed up. "Get your muscles going, but save your energy," I told myself. I rowed into the lake's finger to stay away from the racecourse. I sat for a while watching the current race. I'd be next.

When the starter beckoned to the single scullers to approach the starting line, I rowed over, feeling my nerves kick in. "A little adrenaline is okay," I reassured myself. In those days the women's dash didn't start from a starting dock. Instead the starter lined up the shells free-floating in the water. Doing this was tricky, because all of the shells had to be even. The gun would go off the second that they were. We rowers approached "the line." The starter directed, "Pull forward a stroke. Back up a stroke." We moved a yard forward, then a foot back, trying to hold the line. The starter, eyeing the line, declared us even. Then "Ready! Set!" and the gun went off.

At last. A good start: smooth and quick. Peripherally, I could see that the other rowers also had started well. We surged forward fairly evenly. Within seconds a couple of shells fell off the pace just enough for others to get a lead on them. The water was calm except for the oars digging in deeply on the beginning of the stroke and creating a minimal splash as they came out of the water. Forward on the shell's sliding seat with my oars just skimming the water, I tried to keep the oars from touching the water yet maintain the boat on an even keel. Minimizing friction would maximize each stroke's distance. Halfway through, it became a three-woman race. There were fewer and fewer yards to be covered to gain the lead. I pulled hard for a "big ten," digging long and hard with each stroke to see if I could get ahead. One of the other rowers matched my effort, and we stayed even. The third boat had dropped back just enough that I worried less about its catching me in the final yards.

As the finish line approached, I felt myself running out of gas. I was rowing as hard as I could, or so I thought. My shoulders ached, my legs hurt, and I was breathing so hard that I wondered if I could draw another breath. "This is it. This is it," I kept thinking. "You're almost there. Pick it up." Right. I was dying; how could I pick it up? But I had to if I was going to win the race. In the last few seconds, I had just enough power to edge out the other shell at the finish line. Victory. As I coasted beyond the finish line, my upper body fell forward over my oars and knees in complete exhaustion. In retrospect, I realized that if I had remained sitting up I would have had an easier time breathing because I wouldn't have been crushing my lungs from being slumped over. For a moment or two, I breathed between my legs. Then I had the strength to sit up. I had won the 500-meter dash. I was utterly exhausted and every bit of energy had been spent. With absolute delight and incredible fatigue, I found the strength to row back to the dock.

In addition to winning the race, I set a new national record for the women's 500-meter dash. The contest came down to a fraction of a second. My record would stand for a number of years. Within a week, I sold my shell to another rower with a passion for the sport.

Sometimes we surprise ourselves with what we can do. And the importance of such achievement needn't be measured in years, months, or days. My dash to the finish was measured in a fraction of a second, a fraction that meant win or lose. A person needn't be an athlete to appreciate the value of a second. Just as in rowing, a second can make you a winner as well as a loser. In a second, you can propel yourself to a decision to win in life. In a second, you make that decision to dig deep and put yourself out there. In a second, you can choose to do that something that will keep you from losing the race and make you, in some sense, a winner in the race of a lifetime. In a second, you can miss or grab the opportunity of a moment that may or may not appear again.

God has blessed us with "time." It is how we choose to use that time that matters. Year upon year springs forth wisdom, month upon month brings new life, day upon day brings new opportunity, and second upon second can bring renewed strength. In those last seconds of my rowing race, I had a renewed physical strength because of the days, months, and years of continuous hard work and training toward a goal. But in those last seconds, I am convinced I, too, had a renewed sense of inner drive. To push beyond where you think you can go comes from deep within. That inner strength values each second, because it values the gift of life. Every second is precious in its own way. The moment lost may be difficult to make up. The second is there and then it is gone, but it is still a gift. It is a gift from our Creator. Treasure each bit of life for all the potential it holds. Do not waste a second; life is a gift in which we must invest all our energy, all that is ourselves.

FIVE

The Rain

"A song of praise to our God"
Psalm 40:3

S o far, the weather had been glorious. The sun had been out every day. A
light breeze cooled the air. Our family vacation in the Bahamas was all we
had hoped for. The children played on the beach and swam in the ocean; plus,
for my husband and me, there was time for reading a good book.

We awoke to bright Bahamian sunlight and hardly a cloud in the sky. A
typical day in the islands. After breakfast we headed out for the day's activities.
But by noon, clouds started to build and threatened rain. When the deluge
finally came, it came quickly, and we rushed for cover back at our house. We
plopped onto chairs and the sofa and looked at one another. What would we do
now? No sun, no fun. The game of cards didn't last long. No one was interested
in a board game. So we found ourselves sitting and looking at one another. The
rain poured down in buckets. What now?

A light bulb went off in my head: instead of just sitting inside being miserable,
why not go out and enjoy the rain? Why not put on our bathing suits and play in
the rain? It wasn't cold, only rainy. The kids started for their suits when I had
another idea: let's not bother with bathing suits. Let's just go out in the rain as we
are in our clothes. After all, it's just water, what harm can it do? So out the door
we went, somewhat giddy, dressed in shorts and shirts, but barefoot.

There was usually little traffic on the street in front of our house. We had the road pretty much to ourselves. We found a couple of large puddles. What fun it was to stomp through them, turn around, and stomp back. Our feet sent the water sailing. We splashed one another until we were laughing uncontrollably at the silliness of the whole thing. Here we were, fully dressed, getting wetter by the minute, playing in the rain without a care in the world. At one point I stood with my face to the sky, opened my mouth, and let the rain fill it and run over my face. The drops ran down my cheeks and off my nose. The most glorious feeling. I raised my arms skyward and let the rain run over my whole body. Ahhh . . .

Soon we were soaked to the skin. Our clothes clung to our bodies and dripped water. I wrung out the bottom of my shirt. Our daughters' hair lay flat against their heads, and they looked like drowned rats. Rainwater dripped from my hair onto my face. It tickled as it ran down my cheeks. Again and again we splashed in the puddles. Playing in the rain was far better than building a sandcastle or swimming in the ocean. The novelty stayed with us. We were "crazy" people running around in the rain getting sopping wet. The game ended only when we started to feel cold and the rain started letting up. Laughing hysterically, we had gone back inside to dry off.

I have thought often about our romp in the rain and the pure joy of letting ourselves go to enjoy a gift from God. This spontaneous experience in the physical world is a poignant illustration of a piece of my spiritual life that has become clearer over the last decade. The rain running over every part of me was praise of God. Praise brought forth by experience and not a thing or a person. It is a joy that bubbles from within. Hard to put your finger on other than it seems to fill your very soul and burst out of your pores.

The day had darkened with black thunderheads, yet praise oozed from my soul. The feeling of freshness enveloped my body and ran deep into my heart. I came to it as I was, with no special outfit, just opening myself to the moment. Allowing myself to let go and giving myself over to the wetness as it fell from the sky. Giving myself permission to be swallowed by the moment. As the rain washed over me, I felt cleansed by its life-giving nature. It was as if the wetness brought forth within me praise for God's forgiveness. It was like washing away the sin that consumes us and coming alive again with joy. Life felt renewed. Refreshment had overcome our moment of gloom, all of which brought me to the reality of what true praise feels like. The act of praise gives life. And in this life there is a certain holiness. Romping in the rain, you ask, is holy? As I reflect back now, I believe it is. For in our joy there was a movement from the secular to the spiritual rising from our hearts. There was a joining of hearts with a gift from the Divine. Rain we take for granted, but without it there is no life. God's blessings flow down on us like the rain.

Is giggling and laughing holy? I would suggest that it can be. As we giggled and laughed, our hearts were open to the purest of joys. Closed hearts just don't work in a world in which joy and praise are indispensable. And being with others, the giggles of joy became contagious. God calls us together to enjoy one another, because the passion of the moment of praise spreads quickly from one spirit to another. It spreads almost out of control. I have found pure joy has a way of doing that. We need to turn and embrace it.

I know God has been calling me in my heart to a spirit of praise each day. How do I describe praise from the heart? Yes, there is that feeling in song and worship, in birth and growth, but if I really want to describe it—or better yet, feel it—I take myself back to our romp in the rain, lifting my arms toward the heavens as the rain splashes over me, and offering up my praise to the God of life and joy.

SIX

Skiing

"Do not fear, I will help you"
Isaiah 41:13

Fear of heights had plagued me for years, so I wondered if I could enjoy my next adventure. I had tolerated the cross-country plane trip, but the impending helicopter flight weighed heavily on me. It would be the first of many during my week's vacation in the Canadian Rockies. As I stepped into the helicopter, I became claustrophobic, especially after all the other passengers got in and we were sitting shoulder to shoulder. But somehow being squeezed in like sardines also brought a touch of security. Seated in the middle, I couldn't see the ground as we lifted up and off. As we climbed above the tree line, my muscles tensed. "Hang on," I told myself.

After a short ride, we arrived at the lodge tucked into the mountains. Had it only taken fifteen minutes? It seemed much longer. I felt the tension in my body ease as the helicopter gently touched down on the snow. When I stepped out, I was in immediate awe of the surrounding beauty. These snowcapped mountains were to be our home for the next week.

After dinner, orientation, and a good night's sleep, we found ourselves once more on the helicopter's snow-covered landing pad. Because we would be skiing in remote snowcapped mountains, the possibility of avalanches was always present. With our avalanche call boxes around our necks, we learned how to find someone buried in snow. At first the practice felt like a game, but the reality of the situation soon became clear. This type of skiing could be life-threatening. We had best learn how to turn our receivers on if we became buried. We had best learn how to turn their tracking mode on to find a friend or loved one under multiple feet of snow. I sensed that everyone was attentive and taking the briefing seriously, and this made me feel more at ease, though the possibility of my being buried in an avalanche gave me pause. Life is so easily swept away. Even crossing a city street, you could be struck by a car. Skiing in the Canadian Rockies, you could be buried by an avalanche. In this beautiful, majestic place, we were at nature's mercy. Softening snow could give way, causing a catastrophe. Life is fragile.

By the afternoon we were ready for our first run. With our skis secured to a basket on the side of the helicopter, we climbed in for our first flight up the mountain. This ride felt easier than the first one, but I still chose a seat in the middle so that I couldn't readily look out. We drifted up and over the trees to the mountaintop.

With no defined slope or manicured snow, I had my first experience of cutting through the top crust of the snow on skis. Because of their weight, the men broke through the top layer more easily. I would stay on top of the crust for one turn, but on the next turn would have to fight my way through the crust that I had broken through. It was hard work. I had thought my legs were in good shape from my years of running, but by the end of each descent my quads were sore and protesting.

At the bottom of the run we stood in a clearing waiting for the helicopter to pick us up. My legs were shaky. After what seemed a long wait, I heard the helicopter's rotary blades in the distance. Their "thorping" sound would become familiar over the week. We skiers watched as the copter appeared over the treetops. The snow flew high in every direction as it lightly touched down near us. I had previously been taught to carry my skis over my shoulder, but here we were instructed to drag our skis to the helicopter so that they wouldn't come near the blades. As we boarded, it felt good to sit. We would soon learn that the helicopter's blades were noisy upon approach but uncannily quiet as the copter flew away.

During that week of skiing, the beauty and life of the snowcapped mountains became more and more real for me. On a cloudless day, we skiers stood atop a mountain with a mountainside of virgin snow before us. "Pick your own way down," our guide instructed. The first of our group went, leaving serpentine marks in the glistening white snow. "Let the skis run. Let them do the work. Off you go," our guide said with encouragement.

As I started down, I realized the snow was true virgin powder. As I made the first turn, I felt as if I were floating on a sea of white. I let my skis do the work as I headed for the next turn. They turned and a wall of white flew out from under them. I was keeping the tips of my skis headed down the mountain to make the turns more rhythmic and easier to negotiate. The powdery snow was up to my knees. As I cut through, it flew up my chest and over my shoulders. I bounced through the powder. I was skiing, really skiing. This felt like life to the fullest. When I finally pulled up at the bottom with a less than graceful stop, I felt intensely alive. I looked back up the wall of white snow. There were my tracks, just as in a skiing promotional video. The turns were carved into the pristine snow. The loose, previously flying snow lay to the sides like a rough white blanket. Unfortunately, not all our runs were as glorious, but this one awesome run seemed to make up for others that were less than perfect.

We got to know the ins and outs of deep snow. Around the trees the snow was softer. On one run, I ventured forth toward the trees and soon found myself sliding into a tree well. Before I knew it, I was up to my waist. With nothing firm to stand on, I seemed to sink deeper and deeper the more I tried to get out of the hole. I imagined that quicksand must feel much the same. The more I struggled, the harder I laughed, and the harder I laughed, the more I struggled. When I finally freed myself, my rib cage was as sore from laughing as my legs were from digging out.

Throughout the week of skiing, the helicopter would bring lunch out to us skiers on the slopes. By noon I was tired, having worked hard all morning. My first wish was to sit down, which I did the first day. Sitting on a stump or log was fine, but sitting on snow was a different matter. When we first had lunch in the open snow, I plopped down to get off my feet. Sitting initially felt good, but very soon my bottom got cold and I felt moisture soaking in. Cold liquid started to penetrate my snowsuit. From that day on, I toughed it out, staying on my feet at lunch.

Standing atop a peak in the Canadian Rockies reminded me how small we are. The mountains' majesty was powerful. They stretched as far as I could see.

Massive. Splendid. One day the mountain appeared to drop straight down in front of me. The wall of white below me looked terrifying. My fear of heights kicked in. It was much easier to look out than to look down. Everyone encouraged me; once I dropped over the edge, it wouldn't be that bad. I considered that statement. This wasn't just an edge in front of me but a cliff. My stomach somersaulted. Plain and simple, I was afraid of the cliff in front of me. I edged closer. "Come on, Ingrid, it's all in your mind. You can do this. Just do it." Drawing a deep breath, I pushed forward and slipped over the edge. Amazing. To my great surprise, I made the first turn and was on my way. As I bounced through the powdery snow, my heart raced with the thought that this was life. This was what it was to truly live, using every part of my body, from mind to legs, to conquer this mountain.

My technique having improved with practice, I now felt freedom of movement in the bouncing turns through the snow. As the cold air rushed past my face, I felt free of gravity's pull on my body. As long as I could keep myself upright, I floated above the world's weighty cares. As I skied down the run, my mind drifted into a place that was curiously serene, considering how hard my legs were working. A majestic wonderland of white brought every muscle, every atom, in my mind, heart, and body to life.

I am convinced there are many ways to truly live the life we have been given. I chose to ski the magnificent Canadian Rockies. Others dive to the depths of the sea, create art, perform music, or challenge their mind in research or service. As I reflect on this adventure, it becomes clear to me that it was only when I put aside fear that I could experience life to the full—a life in which I am living beyond the usual expectations, living beyond those things I felt incapable of doing but was willing to try. Note I didn't say I *conquered* a fear. Life is about learning to *manage* our fears, both great and small. I found that I had to set aside my fear of heights by an act of will. To suspend that fear was not easy, most particularly at the beginning. But I saw from this adventure that I needed to deny my fear so I could live. Life is there for the taking. It is easy to get caught in the trap of believing that living consists only in hauling ourselves out of bed every morning. Is Woody Allen correct when he states that 90 percent of living is just showing up? Well, it is more than just showing up. What we need to uncover are those things within us that keep us from really living life to the fullest. Our tendency is to think, *I can't do this. I shouldn't do that. That just isn't me.* Those thoughts may be true in some circumstances, but to experience a life that takes our breath away, we might have to suspend those thoughts and try something new, different, and even remarkable.

When I left the ski lodge at the end of the week, I chose—I repeat, I chose—to ride in the copilot's seat of the helicopter. The entire front of the copter was a big glass bubble, right down to the floor in the front. From my seat I could look up, out, and down. At any given moment, I was surrounded by the total height and depth around us. As we lifted off, I watched the snow landing pad shrink. As I looked out, we climbed up and over the trees. As I looked up, the clouds appeared to be close enough to touch. As we flew out, my eyes widened and took in all the sights around us. I was amazed that I could ride in this part of the copter and not feel my stomach in my throat. The awesomeness of helicopter skiing captivated me one last time.

Life is for the living in all shapes and sizes. God has blessed us with this priceless gift. It is ours for the taking. It is our priceless gift from the Creator of both the lush green valleys and those majestic snow-covered mountaintops.

The fear of heights continues to plague me. As experience has taught me, fear can rob me of a piece of life if I allow it to. The psalmist speaks often of giving your fear over to God. The Old Testament prophet Isaiah echoes that sentiment: "For I, the Lord your God, hold your right hand; it is I who say to you, 'Do not fear; I will help you'" (Isaiah 41:13). Letting go to live can be difficult.

What a blessing it was to ski the Canadian Rockies, to scale the mountains in a helicopter, and stand victorious on the top of a cliff. Putting aside my fears allowed me to hold tightly in my heart the courage and fire of life.

SEVEN

The Parks

"And God saw that it was good."
Genesis 1:10

I n 1989 the US western national parks I had marveled at for years through *National Geographic* magazine came alive for my family. As I reflect on that summer, snapshots like those on picture postcards run through my head. With each photo, a short video plays in my mind, re-creating the events and impressions of awesome beauty that we experienced up close and personal. The memorable moments remain with my family and me as we often recall the adventures of this special time together.

Leaving home in mid-June, we flew to Chicago, where we boarded our Amtrak train headed west. For the children the train ride itself was an adventure. We crowded into small, separate sleeping compartments. It was challenging to maneuver between seats, bunks, and the sink, like six people in a telephone booth all trying to make a call. Their noses pressed to the window, the kids marveled at how different the Midwest was from their home in New England. Flat. Flat. Flat. Cornfields as far as the eye could see. The small towns we passed came and went in a blink. The kids had never seen so many cows. The "walking irrigation systems" which stretched out through field after field fascinated them. It was quite the education for them to travel through farmland. They could see firsthand where their food came from. They saw that the food started somewhere; it didn't just magically materialize on grocery shelves.

The train pulled into our destination of Cut Bank, Montana. My first thought was, "Where's the town?" The train had stopped seemingly in the middle of nowhere. The "town" consisted of a few buildings plus one I would hardly have called a railroad station. Piling off the train, loaded with our suitcases, we stood on the side of the road. Our travel agent had told us that we'd be able to get a taxi to our hotel. There were no taxis in sight. From the emptiness of the space, I couldn't imagine a taxi within miles. What now? Along came a black pickup truck. I guess we looked lost and out of place, because the burly driver stopped and asked if we needed help. My husband, Bill, being the man he is said, "Sure." The kids looked doubtful. But when the driver told them to hop into the truck bed with two huge German shepherds, their faces lit up. We piled the luggage in first. Then the kids jumped in. Cool! Bill helped me up into the cab and gently pushed me toward the driver, to the middle of the seat. The first thing that caught my eye was a large rifle hanging on a gun rack behind the front seat. Great! Bill climbed in and slammed the door, and we were off to the hotel. Our "cowboy" driver turned out to be very nice and most accommodating.

We were to pick up our newly purchased van at a dealership in Cut Bank. This van was to be our mode of travel for our trip. When Bill had asked the dealer when and how we could pick up the van, the dealer answered matter-of-factly, "I'll leave the keys in it for you." That had stunned us. A dealer leaving keys in a new car when no papers had been signed? How trusting can you get? That evening a person from the hotel gave us a lift to the dealership. Sure enough, there was the van with the keys. The next morning we drove back to the dealership, signed the papers of ownership, and started toward Glacier National Park.

We stayed at the park's lodge, which was rustic and beautiful, just what you'd expect in a western lodge. I especially remember the clouds during our stay. They rolled in and out, off the mountaintops. The peaks, a wide variety of grays and whites, disappeared in a moment and then slowly reappeared as the clouds crawled away to reveal their snow-blanketed majesty. As we traveled the park's historic Going-to-the-Sun Road, past glacier lakes and towering mountains, we were in awe of the incredible beauty.

We hiked the trails one afternoon and found snow on many parts. A silence of wonder and mystery surrounded us in the cold. At one point we rounded a corner to find the trail completely blocked by snow. It was mid-June, but the trail was impassable. Jonathan and Brooks took the opportunity to throw snowballs at each other. A snowball fight in June. A kick for the boys. As I reflect on the magnificent glaciers that we saw, I treasure those moments and hope my children do, too. Before long the glaciers may be gone.

Again we were on the road, to our next destination of Yellowstone National Park. Flipping through my mental snapshots of Yellowstone, I see us soaking wet. Bill suggested we go for a hike to take in the beauty around us. We had hiked for quite a distance when the heavens opened up and rain came down in buckets. Believe me, we hiked back faster than we hiked out! We looked like six half-drowned puppy dogs, clothes stuck to our bodies, hair stuck to our heads, limbs shivering from the cold. Our cabin had never looked so good.

In the middle of our stay at Yellowstone, we were sitting at breakfast stocking up on carbohydrates for the day when a commotion arose. It seemed to be coming from the front door. We turned and looked. The kids shouted, "There's a moose!" A moose was indeed standing on the front doorstep looking in at us. Was he here for breakfast? We all laughed. He seemed unfazed by our presence. This huge creature stood for a long time, swinging his head back and forth as if enjoying the show of humans. We stared in amazement. Then, as calmly as he had arrived, he turned and strode away. But that was not our first encounter with the park's large beasts. We'd encountered bison crossing the road and causing a traffic jam. Christina had dared her father to get out of the van and shoo the bison across more quickly. Fortunately, Bill had more sense than to take up his daughter's dare. Now a moose had joined us for breakfast, up close and personal in the wild West.

A trip to the western parks is incomplete without a visit to Old Faithful. We walked through geyser fields before reaching Old Faithful. The kids were intrigued by the steam rising from the ground. They gazed with wide eyes at the eerie mist rising into the air and evaporating into nothingness. Even more impressive for us were the mineral springs bubbling at the surface in many different colors. The kids were delighted to learn that the lighter-colored springs were the hotter springs. They then made a game of seeing who could find the hottest geysers. When we reached Old Faithful, I was a bit disappointed by the commercialism. This wonder of nature, which I'd seen in *National Geographic*, was surrounded by park benches and people, who sat and stood. My kids ran around. Everyone was waiting for Old Faithful to shoot up. We waited. And waited. Finally, the geyser shot up in the most beautiful spray. What a show it was. Spontaneous applause rang out.

A final note on Yellowstone. As we drove within the park, we viewed burned mountainsides. We saw the devastation caused by the prior year's forest fires. It was heartrending to think of all the beauty the land had lost. So much destruction of nature's wonders. We drove through a section of burned mountain. Even the children's faces turned sad. It was hard to look at the destruction, but every so often I could pick out a bit of green within the charred timbers. Such green stood out like an emerald in the mud, shining with the promise of new life. It would be a long time before the mountain would return to its former self, but it would happen because of the wonders of nature. God saw creation and said it was good. May it continue to be so.

We piled back into our van and made our way from Yellowstone to Grand Teton National Park. Here we would whitewater raft on the Snake River. After much preparation and a drive to the put-in place on the river, we loaded into our raft with six other visitors and a guide. We Barretts claimed the stern. Seated on the sides of the raft, we were off. Secretly, I was glad we all were wearing life jackets. The water was calm, unthreatening, but the day had just begun. Soon the river started to run fast. Swept along, we got into the rhythm of the bubbling, flowing current. I watched our guide with fascination as he single-handedly managed our raft with two long oars. He had obviously done this many times.

After a stop for lunch, we climbed back on board and headed for the "real" rapids. "Hold on," the guide commanded. I saw churning white water just ahead. It bubbled, splashed, and beat against the large rocks in the middle of the river. The rocks glistened in the sunlight. An opening between the boulders to the right offered a way through. I grabbed the safety rope running down the raft's center. With trepidation, I looked around at my children to make sure that they, too, were holding onto the rope. "Hold on!" I ordered them. There was nothing but smiles and wide eyes as we approached the falls and rapids. I saw the joy and excitement in my children's faces. They were like kids in a candy store with all the money in the world to spend on their favorite treats. The raft's bow hit the whitewater and the thrill began.

The guide held us on a straight course as the raft began to be battered about. To the left. To the right. As we hit the middle of the rapids, the raft became a rollercoaster. The bow flew into the air, clearing the water as the stern fell. Wow! In rebound the stern catapulted off the water and into the air. Wow! The kids screamed with delight. My head swung around from one child to another, making sure they still were with us. I was praying I wasn't going to lose one of them. Christina looked like she was riding a bucking bronco. Next to her, Brooks was screaming with a wide-open mouth. With eyes of pure delight, Elizabeth and Jonathan were hunkered down in their hooded foul-weather gear. The water splashed us in the boat, and all around us. The thrill was one to remember always. Sopping wet, we emerged into calmer water. Smiles all around, we bantered back and forth about those few minutes of pure ecstatic adventure. What delight I felt in being able to give my children such excitement!

We drove on to Salt Lake City, where we toured the State House and Temple Square in all their grandeur. Then, with a bit of groaning from the kids, we found our way to Great Salt Lake. "What's so great about a lake?" they groaned. They'd had a wild ride on the Snake River. How could a placid lake compare? But when we got to the lake, it was amazing. Our side of the lake was very shallow. People had waded out quite far, and the water came only to their thighs. People floated serenely. We were about to discover the properties of salt in water. Even I, who had never been able to float, lay back in the water as if I were supported by a soft, warm cushion. Like corks, we playfully bobbed around each other on our backs.

From floating we moved to horseback riding at Bryce Canyon as our journey continued. I had unsuccessfully tried my hand at riding when I was in elementary school, and Christina and Elizabeth had taken some riding lessons at summer camp. That was the extent of our family's experience with horses. But a trail ride was on the itinerary for Bryce. As my kids stood at the railing of the corral, their faces shone with excitement but also conveyed some doubt about this adventure. Upon arriving at the canyon, we had seen its beauty and its high ridges and cliffs. We all were wondering, "Where, exactly, will we be riding? What kind of horses will we get?" I think we all were hoping for nice, calm, easy-to-ride horses. I certainly was.

The ride was thrilling. The trails took us along ridges, some dropping off hundreds of feet to the canyon floor below. Many of the ridges dropped off on both sides of the trail. That was frightening. My fear of heights rode with me the whole way. Whenever we descended to a lower trail, I breathed more easily. I watched my children as their horses lumbered along. The height didn't seem to bother the children at all. "Good for them," I thought. They could really enjoy the beauty of the cliffs and endless ridges carved out of the landscape over time. When we got back to the corral, I thought, "Not a bad warm-up for our ride down the Grand Canyon." Next we headed to Zion.

Zion's red rocks and roads were incredibly beautiful. We hiked the trails that wound their way through this magnificent landscape. With wide eyes we took in the natural arches carved by the weather from the rock and the lovely red soil. The magnificent rocks and cliffs, in their colorful wardrobe, were among the many wonders of nature and our national parks that Bill and I had wanted our children to see, touch, and feel in their bones. A treasure of God's creation. "And God saw that it was good" (Genesis 1:10).

After Zion's solitude and quiet came Las Vegas. What a change! We all felt it as soon as we hit the strip. We had traveled for two weeks through nature's vastness, untouched by human hands, to a place of nothing but people. All of the children, even our youngest, Brooks, were struck by the lights, the casinos, the marriage chapels on every corner. They loved the busy excitement in the air. I, however, felt claustrophobic. Too much. Too many people. Too artificial. As I wandered through a windowless casino, I thought, "You can't even tell the time of day." People gambled twenty-four hours a day. I sat in front of a slot machine to give this entertainment a try. Being frugal, I chose the nickel slots. Big-time gambling for me. Without the knowledge of the casino's management, my two daughters had entered the casino with me. After all, we'd be there only a short time. I fed the machine nickel after nickel. The lights blinked and the machine dinged. I had won! Next thing I knew, I was on a winning streak. The nickels kept tumbling out into the tray. Clang, clang, clang. Christina and

Elizabeth cheered me on. This was fun! Thinking back on this one winning streak in my extremely limited experience of casinos, I can appreciate gambling's seductiveness and the hold of winning money. My daughters' cheering was cut short when two security guards approached and politely told me that the girls must leave because they were underage. Just as well. The statistics indicate that I soon would have started to lose. Better to leave with some gains, however small. After all I was only playing the nickel slots!

As we drove away from the lights of Vegas, we headed for the high point of our vacation in the national parks. Our entire trip had been planned around a mule ride down into the Grand Canyon. Brooks wasn't big enough to ride a mule, so he and Bill would take a plane ride through the canyon, a ride that would prove spectacular and memorable. Christina, Elizabeth, Jonathan, and I would saddle up for the ride of a lifetime.

In the afternoon, we walked out onto one of the scenic platforms for our first view of the Grand Canyon. Disbelief embraced us. An indescribably magnificent array of colors reflected off the canyon walls. The canyon's magnitude seemed unreal. It took my breath away. Silence and majesty, time and creation grabbed me as never before. I stood frozen in wonder. The faces of my children, too, showed wonder. The feeling lasted only a minute or two before we began to acclaim the sight, but in those moments we were touched to our innermost being of our created selves. The reality of being there was so much better than all the photos of the canyon I had seen over the years. This was the real thing. Wow!

Early the next morning, we walked to the corral to begin our mule ride. The mules wandered about in the enclosure as we inspected them curiously. Our transportation for the day. They didn't look very smart; they walked around with a dazed look. I was assigned a mule named Helen Keller, because she was blind in one eye. I'd been a bit tentative about this ride from the start. Now I was having serious doubts. Before we started down the trail, our guide had instructions for us. Whenever we stopped, we should turn our mules out away from the canyon wall, so they could see where they were. The mules were not to trot, but to walk at all times. "Keep up with the mule in front of you, but don't get too close. Remember the mules know exactly where they're going and what they're doing." Then came the clincher: if anyone screamed on the trail's first turn, they would be brought back up and not be allowed to continue the ride.

What had I gotten my family into? The instructions didn't faze Christina, Elizabeth, and Jonathan, who mounted up, ready to go.

The mule train reached the trail's first hairpin turn. I watched as the mules in front of me lumbered around the corner and the riders swayed in their saddles. As Helen took me around that first curve with a bumping and swaying, I swallowed hard to contain the scream I felt inside. I was so scared. The trail was so narrow, the curve so sharp, and the drop so steep that my heart skipped a beat or two. I thought, "This is going to be a really long day." I hoped that my trust in Helen would grow. Meanwhile, my kids soaked up the thrill. The girls beamed, and Jonathan rode his mule like a cowboy. Good for them!

We lumbered down the narrow, dusty trail. The canyon wall was often there at our left shoulders while inches away on the right the cliff dropped off hundreds of feet. As the hours passed, all of us riders felt increasingly at one with our mules. By the time we reached Indian's Garden, everyone was enjoying the awesome adventure. The temperature rose throughout the morning. When we finally took a break, Elizabeth was so hot that we had to pour cold water over her to keep her reasonably comfortable. Her wet shirt was a relief. We all took advantage of the large boulders that provided the only shade at our resting point.

The ride up the trail proved far less frightening. Relaxing, I could more fully appreciate the scenery near and far. Gazing across the canyon to the other side offered a spectacular view. Looking up, looking down, we were swallowed up by millions of years etched in rock. A few hours of riding within the canyon seemed so insignificant compared to the canyon's millions of years. By midafternoon we arrived safely back at the rim. The mules had been great. My kids had been great. We'd always hold this ride in our memories and hearts.

As I reflect upon the Grand Canyon in all its splendor, I'm overpowered by creation's re-creating itself over and over, ever so slowly. I'm overpowered by the forces of wind, rain, and sun and by the canyon's vastness and my smallness. Years later the spirituality of my ride in the Grand Canyon, and all the beauty of the western parks, engulfs me.

Paul wrote to the Colossians, "As God's chosen ones, holy and beloved, clothe yourselves with compassion, kindness, humility, meekness, and patience" (Colossians 3:12). In the vastness of the West, one cannot but feel humility, but also a feeling of meekness. Meekness is not to suggest weakness but the understanding that we are called to walk in the shadow of where God keeps watch over His own. To know meekness is a walk in a quiet godliness. The Grand Canyon brought home for me the realization that being meek means seeking one's self in relationship to God and God's call, and realizing God's greatness. The Grand Canyon and all the other parks renewed that journey of faith within me.

From the Grand Canyon we traveled to Vail, Colorado, as well as visiting such places as Four Corners National Monument, Mexican Hat in Utah, and Telluride in Colorado. What a treat when we arrived in Vail. As a family, we had skied in Vail for many years, but we'd never seen it in summer. The previously snowcapped mountains had changed their wardrobe to green and the brilliant colors of wildflowers. Looking up the mountainside, the kids picked out their favorite ski runs, now brightly colored. We tubed on the river, rode the gondola to the mountain's top, and hiked the trails down. On the way down, the kids would run ahead, yelling "Look at me skiing!" as they pretended to swish to a stop.

An airplane ride from Denver to home brought our adventure to an end. We were tired but exhilarated. To live and breathe the vastness and wonder of the western parks was an adventure always to be remembered.

When each of my children reached age sixteen, Bill took them on the adventure of their choice, a time for just the two of them. Each child chose to return to nature's awesomeness. Christina chose rafting down the Colorado River through the Grand Canyon, Elizabeth chose a Wyoming cattle drive, Jonathan chose climbing the Grand Teton, and Brooks chose a week exploring the Galapagos Islands. These times were very special for father and child. I vicariously relive these adventures whenever I go to the third floor of our house. There on the wall are four poster-size photos of each pair on their joint adventure. My heart is warmed by these memories, and I feel truly blessed by God the creator.

EIGHT

9/11

"The man became a living being."
Genesis 2:7

How can I ever forget the day? How can anyone ever forget where they were when they first heard the news? Each of us, I'm sure, has their own story to tell about that fateful day.

When I woke up and drove to work, the day seemed unremarkable. I had decided to take the back way to the highway, to avoid the traffic around school entrances. I was on autopilot as I wound my way through the towns. As always, I had turned on the news radio station to hear traffic reports and weather. After fifteen minutes I'd caught all that information, so I switched the channel to my favorite oldies station. The disc jockeys exchanged the usual banter. Annoying, senseless banter. But I loved the '60s music, so I continued to listen. I was on Wellesley Street in Weston, Massachusetts, driving north toward Route 128, passing through neighborhoods before reaching Route 30. I was not speeding, just keeping pace with the cars in front of me, making good time; I would not be late for work. The sunshine wove through the trees that were just starting to turn to their fall colors, creating patches of light and dark on the road. Sunshine would flash on my windshield, bright in my eyes. Then I would return to the darkness of shadow. Little did I know such would be that day.

Land and Water

About ten minutes before 9:00 a.m., the radio announcer broke into the regular program with the first news of an event that would change our lives forever. His tone was somewhat matter-of-fact but with an undercurrent of incredulity. Reportedly a plane had hit the World Trade Center. What? Was this an accident? Had a plane veered off course and crashed into one of the Twin Towers? How had this freak thing happened? Startled, I drove on, intent on every word of the announcer who soon reported that a second plane had hit the second Twin Tower. What? I understood what he was reporting but couldn't accept the news as reality. I know the Twin Towers; I know New York City well, but this whole thing was surreal. An indescribably unsettled emotion pierced me and went right to my heart. If this was true, think of all those people who potentially had lost their lives. It couldn't be true.

I speed-dialed home on my cell phone. On the second ring my husband picked up. "Turn on the TV," I said urgently. "Planes have hit the World Trade Center in New York!"

"What?" He sounded disbelieving.

"Turn on the TV." I hung up and continued listening to the radio. My husband later told me that he spent the rest of the day sitting in front of the TV. By the time I got to work, the music station was reporting all the information about what was unfolding in New York City. The final half hour of my drive to work is a blank. Like the rest of the world I was in shock, feeling the tremors of tragedy.

When I got to the church, my secretary was already working. I blurted out, "Did you hear the news?"

"What news?" she asked. "I've been here at the office since eight thirty."

"Planes have hit the World Trade Center."

Her face was a mix of blank disbelief and deep concern. "What?"

I repeated what I'd heard on the radio. We talked briefly, and I remembered that I had a TV, rarely used, in my office. What had previously been little more than a piece of stored furniture acquired new meaning. The television became my window on a world that had seemingly gone mad. Remote in hand, I turned it on. My eyes were fixed on the screen. The pictures coming out of Manhattan were beyond words. Then came images of the third plane crashing into the Pentagon. What? These first pictures out of New York City and DC would be played over and over as the day unfolded, and also in the weeks, months, and years since that fateful Tuesday, September 11, 2001. Who has not seen them?

When the terrifying reality set in, I phoned my parents, who were in Manhattan. I dialed their number. The phone rang a few times before my mother picked up. I didn't realize how lucky I had been to get through; soon after, all communications in and out of the city shut down. "Are you okay, Mom? Is Dad okay?"

My mother assured me she was all right because she lived uptown, but her day had just started to unfold. She didn't realize how life would slowly draw to a halt as the tragedy engulfed the entire city.

"What about Dad?"

"He's safe."

My father's office isn't far from the World Trade Center. I would later learn that he had been on the subway when the first plane hit. When he emerged from underground, the chaos on the street baffled him. "What's all this?" A passerby told him. He moved quickly to his building to get off the street. He called my mother to make sure she was okay and let her know he was okay. But that, too, was just the beginning of a horrendous day.

My mother and I talked about Manhattan and the surrealism of what had happened. Although deeply upset and concerned, we remained calm. Details of the horror were just beginning to unfold. United Airlines Flight 93 hadn't yet crashed in Pennsylvania. We didn't talk long and agreed to check on each other later in the day. But when I tried to reach my mother later in the morning, in the afternoon, and in the evening, I couldn't get through. I was caught in the dark like everyone else, trying desperately to get in contact with loved ones. The phone circuits went silent. The world turned black.

I don't remember in what order the next things happened in my life, because it was such a time of inner and outer turmoil. Soon, video of the Pentagon ablaze and news of Flight 93 came over the TV. There were more pictures of Washington, DC while we watched replays, again and again, of the planes hitting the Twin Towers. Before our eyes the South Tower collapsed. Then the North Tower. Lower Manhattan was crumbling. These were really tough pictures to watch. I had a hard time imagining how truly heart-wrenching these pictures were for the families and friends who lost loved ones in the planes and buildings that day. I can reach deep inside and try to feel the pain, but because I knew no one well who lost their life that day, I cannot truly appreciate the ripping pain and anguish. As the pictures flashed across the TV screen, I don't think I truly comprehended the implications of what had occurred. That would come later through reflection and conversation.

My TV watching was interrupted by a phone call from a parishioner. A meeting of the finance committee was scheduled for that night. Would we still have it? We got distracted from her question about the meeting and began discussing the terrorist attack. She had fairly high clearance with the government but was not authorized to share all that she knew, so I obtained no new information. She said she might not be able to attend the meeting because of her work's involvement in the unfolding events. In fact, she might not be allowed to leave her building for security reasons. Planes were being forced to land all across the country. "Talk to you later," she hurriedly said before hanging up. We went ahead and held the meeting that night. Maybe we thought the whole thing was just going to magically go away if we went on with our plans. Maybe it was our way of denying all that happened. Maybe we just couldn't look at one more picture of planes flying into buildings, towers collapsing in a billow of smoke, or people gasping for air and running for their lives. These images remain etched in my head and cut into my heart. But who hasn't felt such pain from that day?

The door to the church now opened, and my daughter entered crying out, "Can you believe it? Can you believe it?" Elizabeth was close to a state of panic. She worked in Boston. Were planes going to crash into Boston's skyscrapers as well? Were Boston's buildings also going to collapse? She had to get out of the city and stay out. She flung herself onto my couch and caught her breath. We talked, rehashing everything we had heard. Yes, Grandfather and Grammie were okay, I assured her.

The TV continued to spit out news, so we turned our attention to its pictures and voices. The horror of the terrorist's attack was sinking in. We were scared and certainly didn't know what would happen next; the uncertainty overwhelmed us.

Reflecting back on that day, it was the sense of fear and uncertainty that struck right to my core. Everyone likes to know what is going to happen next.

Control is important to us. At the very least, we like to believe we have some control over what is going to occur. Whether we are aware of it or not, we like to keep our lives from going dangerously chaotic. When you stop to reflect, most particularly on a situation that is difficult or causing pain, you will find at the core, control. Control comes up again and again as I work through all the dynamics of life. On 9/11 control of life was slipping away from me. Control of life had slipped away for thousands. Even those in high positions seemed powerless. Our president disappeared from view. The terrorists wielded the control, and that was very scary, short term and long term.

When I returned home that afternoon, my husband still was glued to the TV. He confessed he couldn't pull himself away. Although he had seen the day's events replayed over and over, he was still in shock. The haunting question kept repeating: how could this happen?

After dinner I left for my meeting, trying desperately to think about something else. At the meeting we were all numb as we sat around the table trying to complete the order of business. The day's horrors were painted on our faces. We prayed. We prayed long and hard. We needed to connect to one another, to those who had lost their lives, to grieving families and friends, and to those wandering about, carrying hope in their hearts that their loved one would be found alive. We needed to connect to God. We needed to connect with our faith in God's grace and love.

We all have stories to tell about the events of that day. Many of these stories didn't unfold until the next day when communications had been restored. Some found loved ones to be safe, and, sadly, others found loved ones had perished in the death traps of collapsing buildings. Still others had to continue the painful process of waiting and then waiting some more.

In the following days, I learned what my brother and father had experienced in their downtown office close to the Twin Towers. I remember my brother's words.

"When the towers came down and the gigantic cloud of dust and smoke engulfed lower Manhattan," he said, "it rose up the side of my building and swallowed up the windows." At that moment he had a flashback to Vietnam. All the horrors of war came flooding back. I can only imagine what it must have felt like as he relived that terror and horror of attack.

By midafternoon my brother and father decided to make their way uptown. They had to walk. All downtown traffic had been at a standstill since early morning. They hoped to get far enough uptown to hitch a ride from someone. We've all seen the pictures of people choking from the smoke, dust, and debris with tear-streaked faces of ash. My brother and father ventured out into that. To protect themselves from the ash in the air, they covered their heads and faces with wet towels. As I picture these two men dressed in business suits groping through the ashen darkness, I am still scared for them. But they did what they had to do to get home, and I realize how lucky they were that they could find their way through people, debris, and chaos. I admire them for facing that challenge, though their challenge was not as great as so many others. But each New Yorker, in his or her own way, fought to make it through the day and be united with family or loved ones.

To be alive took on new meaning that day. "Then the Lord God formed man from the dust of the ground and breathed into his nostrils the breath of life; and the man became a living being" (Genesis 2:7). And in all that God created, God saw it and declared it to be very good. Life is a gift. Life is precious. Life is good. Too often we forget that until it is swept away from us. On 9/11 lives were swept away from us through acts of terror that we still don't quite comprehend. Sadly, the gift of life was used as a weapon of terror. That cuts to the very heart and soul; it tears apart the very inner being. The conflict and sadness in my heart overwhelmed my thoughts the following day. I wept inwardly and outwardly for the people who were lost. And there were far too many, as the days afterward proved.

As a pastor, I have often been asked about the presence of evil on that day. Surely we saw it center stage. Like the dust and ash, evil seemed to swallow us up. I found myself asking: so this is evil? What is evil? For me, evil is about intentionality and the abuse of power. It is the intentionality and abuse of power that was transformed into a weapon against humanity—a weapon created for destruction both of our physical world as well as the human body, heart, and soul.

In the cross, Christians see God's struggle against evil. In Christ's resurrection, they see God's promise of final victory over evil. I ask myself, "Want to know what evil is, Ingrid?" Look at the Holocaust, think of genocide throughout our world, look to 9/11. Remember all the horrific pictures from September 11. Remember the ash and dust, the crying and wailing. Remember all the lives forever changed. Why put the label of evil on it? Because it was an intentional act of sheer scorn for God's gift of life—purposefully and carefully planned to take from individuals as many loved ones as possible. To strike terror in ordinary people. To have that terror fester in hearts. But it is my confidence in the sovereignty of a living God's love and grace that empowers me to move against evil and trust that evil will not be the victor.

As I drove to my church the next day, I knew I had to do something to fight that evil and return to the God of love and grace. Many churches had conducted services the evening of 9/11. By the time I got to my church the next morning, I knew that I, too, must offer the comfort, healing, and peace of God, whom I knew to be the good giver of life. I asked my secretary to inform a couple of my deacons that I would be offering a 10:00 a.m. service and to ask them to please spread the word to the congregation. I had no idea who the deacons would call or if they would even make phone calls.

Then I went into my office, closed the door, and prayed. I dove into my books of liturgies seeking words of healing. I reworked prayers and readings in an effort to capture the emotions I was feeling and reach out to people I knew had to be hurting as much as I was. The service turned out to be simple, but I believe it offered the words that people needed to hear.

We opened the church's doors at 9:45. The doors faced a busy route through town. Ordinarily, most of the traffic kept moving. Most passersby probably didn't even notice the church anymore. Like many of today's pastors, I wondered if my church was invisible. I entered the sanctuary and sat in the middle of the front pew. I gazed at the cross and stained-glass window on the altar wall. The sunlight shone through the window's colors, making the image of Christ glow radiantly. The cross stood in solitary silence, reminding me of the meaning of my faith. I wondered what others were thinking and what they would do the "morning after." Was their reaction the same as mine? I expected maybe a handful of people to interrupt hectic schedules to attend a service of remembrance and healing. Would they take time from work or pull themselves away from the TV? Who would turn to their faith or reach deep to find a faith that might help them cope? I was soon to find out.

I sat there in the silence by myself. I prayed and reflected, questioned and tried to reason. I heard someone enter. Selfishly, I mumbled to myself, "Good, at least I have one person who cares." Another person entered and took a seat. Then two more. I didn't turn around to see who had entered or how many. As the minutes clicked off to the top of the hour, I heard more and more people enter the sanctuary. I realized the pews were filling up with people seeking something. Those fifteen minutes were fifteen of the most powerful moments of my ministry.

Just after 10:00, I walked up the altar steps to the pulpit. When I turned around, I was blown away by the sea of faces. The sanctuary of my little church was almost full. I saw not only familiar congregants but many strangers. It was only in their faces that I glimpsed a familiarity. All were alike in their horror, fear, and grief. All were seeking God's goodness and love to heal their wounds. They had come to give thanks for the preciousness of life and mourn its loss through terrorism.

Where is faith? Who knows where it resides in most of us most of the time. It seems hidden and unimportant most days. It is taken for granted and only removed from the shelf and dusted off when we need it. It's like good glassware on the cupboard's upper shelf, stored away for special occasions, pretty to look at but too fragile to be used on a regular basis. How sad. Well, all these people sitting out there in my sanctuary that Wednesday had reached high to try to retrieve that precious glassware of faith, to drink from it and hope that it would nourish and heal. As I stood before them, the silence seemed deafening. Everyone was looking to me. Prayers raced through my head: "Give me strength, give me wisdom, help me to speak a word of your comfort and peace, Dear God."

As I offered prayers and words of solace and remembrance, I looked into tears and disbelief, numbness and stares into nothingness. I prayed that in my own small way I was helping them to connect with God and that God was working in all mystery to heal and restore. After the service, everyone departed in silence. The initial fifteen minutes before the service grew into forty-five minutes of the most powerful minutes of my ministry. If ever I have felt the power of God's presence, it was most certainly in that service.

As with the question of evil, so many people have asked me, *where was God on 9/11?* Was God there at all? I, too, struggled with that question. The terrorists wanted to drag us away from a God of love and send us crashing into a state of darkness.

For many, 9/11 was a time and place of learning and testing of faith. My trust in God and Christ became paramount. Relationships became key. That day all of us reached out for someone. It was in those moments of conversation and relationship with others and God that I felt His very presence. I felt God weeping like the rest of us, reaching out to keep us from crashing in utter despair. In the faces of those who survived against all odds, in the faces of those who dug and searched, in the faces of all those people who wept for others, and in the faces of those who did what they could, no matter how monumental or how little, I saw God's presence and sensed His grace breathing life back into each of us.

Like so many others, I wonder how can I ever forget that day?

NINE

The Beach

"More majestic than the waves of the sea"
Psalm 93:4

The colors shone in brilliant contrasts. The horizon divided the view into halves. The waves lapped gently, and the breeze rustled through the trees. The quiet was restful, thankfully. No one talking, no radios playing, no cars whizzing by, just the soothing background sounds of nature. I pulled a beach chair over the sand halfway to the ocean's edge. With an inner sigh of contentment, I slid into the chair. My toes dug into the white sand, warm and smooth as fresh-cooked mashed potatoes. Running my feet through the sand always has given me great pleasure. I dug a small hole with them, planting myself for my stay on the beach. As I slouched in the beach chair, my body and mind relaxed, and wondrous reflections on the beach began.

The bright blue sky first held my attention. Why does the sky always look so much bluer at the ocean's edge? Nudged by a soft breeze, small puffy clouds floated slowly by. Captivated, I looked for recognizable shapes. Was that a dog? A face looking down at me? As the clouds drifted, they seemed to purposely morph from one shape to another. Their fluffy delicacy drew me skyward. As I watched the rolling clouds from the beach, I viewed them as a pleasing contrast to the blue sky, thereby enhancing the beauty of the heavens. Awe inspiring. One large cloud soon covered the sun. The darkness was minimal, but the aura felt different as the sun's heat dissipated. How easily sunlight is broken or lost. With this image, my spiritual musing took hold.

Light is precious. Light holds a life-giving message. In our lives how easily and quickly we move from light to darkness. In the morning we rise to the sunlight of a new day, but it takes only one phone call or one rude comment to cast a cloud over that light. The voice on the other end has troubling news or offends us. Darkness descends on the spirit. Where has the light gone? Why do clouds of darkness cover us? When large black clouds appear on the horizon, I know I must soon leave the beach. They signal rain, warning me to run from my relaxing spot. Darkness in our lives causes us to seek shelter and comfort. It signals an alarm within us that all is not well. Our sole desire becomes escaping the darkness and returning to the light.

My eye caught the clouds floating just above the horizon. Clouds seem to get lost as they meet the ocean. I wondered at the horizontal line running across my view. "How far out is it?" I mused. This day there was nothing between me and the horizon—no boats, planes, or people. Only the blues of the ocean lay beneath the horizon. Sitting on the beach gazing at the horizon, I could appreciate why people once believed the world was flat. The sea appears flat, as if you would fall off the edge if you ventured far enough out. But we know better. God's oceans stretch around our good earth, without beginning or end.

As I pondered the seeming edge of the world, I was awed by the sense of distance. With nothing out there but water, my depth perception was askew. The horizon was so far away, yet it seemed to approach me. It beckoned and embraced me. For one instant, the horizon and I were joined together as wonders of God's creation. The water's myriad colors were beautiful beyond words. Deep blues blended into light blues, which blended into aquas and sandy blues. The colors created a mosaic platform for the small whitecaps and swells.

As the ocean nears the beach, its movement becomes more apparent. At the horizon the ocean appears calm and windless, but as it stretches to the land's edge, swells are visible. The water rhythmically changes height. The ocean seems timeless and flowing. Its movement has a calming effect. While swimming along a sandy ocean floor, I've seen the movement of the grasses growing from the bottom. They sway in time with the ocean's currents. I dance with them. Swaying left, swaying right, the grasses and I keep time with each other.

My thoughts return to the surface. The ocean stretches out again before me. I love the water. I recall spending much of my youth on the water, whose blues seem to possess a life-giving force. As I look out at the vast ocean, I consider places and people starved for water. All this water, yet much of the world is parched. Crops dying. People suffering because they lack fresh water. Where have we gone wrong? Water has within it the power of life. Why haven't we respected that?

So much water. Such a gigantic ocean. The enormity overtakes me. How small I feel. My mind drifts over the water. As I stare out, I rehash all the "stuff" of the last weeks and months running chaotically around within me. Disconnected thoughts skip from one scene to another. And then, all that "stuff" begins to vanish from my consciousness. Finally, to my delight, my mind is empty. I am concentrating on absolutely nothing. Peace and serenity. The water tranquilizes me into a state of relaxation; it runs through my body, touching my inner soul.

I bury my toes deep in the sand, again and again. Only on the beach do I realize how much my toes feel. Most of the time they are shoved into socks and shoes and merely maintain my balance when I walk. But in smooth, fine sand, they absorb nature's softness.

I came to the beach, book in hand, intending to read. With a good story as my companion, I would soak in the sand and ocean. But when I returned to the book, the pages couldn't hold my attention. Over the top of the book were the blues of the sea and sky, and they drew me back. Back, back. To the distant horizon. I didn't resist and just let myself drift into the ocean. "More majestic than the thunders of mighty waters, more majestic than the waves of the sea, majestic on high is the Lord!" (Psalm 93:4). Such a feeling overtakes me.

Sitting in the bright sunshine, I became aware of a soft breeze floating in from the ocean. It caressed my face. How the wind has a will of its own. A puff here, a puff there. Up and down it moves, picking up the rhythm of the waves lapping on the beach. My thoughts adopted the same rhythm and flow, moving from randomness to spiritual contemplation of the ocean's vastness and on to peaceful nothingness. The emptying of self refreshes as much as the breeze.

Ultimately, the beautiful vastness overtook me. Sea and sky seemed endless. Creation stretched before me in one of her finest wardrobes. People often ask me, "How do you know there's a God?" Perhaps they never have sat within creation's vastness. The enormity of the universe sinks home on the beach. That scene before me was most truly created for us by a loving hand so that we may marvel. Creator God spoke, and the seas and skies appeared. God continues to create within us the knowledge of Himself through the wonders I viewed while sitting on the beach.

How do I know there is a God? I don't believe I *know* there is God as much as I *feel* there is God. I feel it in the breeze stroking my face. I feel it in the sand squishing between my toes. I view it in the brilliant colors of ocean and sky. I watch it in the fluffiness of the clouds drifting by. Only as people feel the presence of God do they believe in His power and existence. I am present on the beach as one small being in the vastness of creation. God has stretched out His creation before me for wonder, for amazement, and most truly so I can personally know this God who cares so much for me and for all. Feeling wonder, I feel God.

II

Body and Mind

TEN

The Window

"For remember I am with you always."
Matthew 28:20

I can't remember where we had been or what we had done, but I do remember pulling into our driveway. Four years old, I had lived in this house all my life. These young childhood memories are not all clear. I can put together only bits and pieces. I remember now what the living room looked like, and the kitchen, dining room, and hallway. I can't clearly remember the stairs to the second floor, but the placement of the bedrooms remains familiar. The driveway was to the right of the house, and the backyard was a good play area. From those early years one incident has replayed through my mind, over and over again.

With the car parked in the driveway, my parents, older brother, and I climbed out and headed to our front door. There's nothing particularly unusual about this except for the fact that when my parents reached the door, they discovered they couldn't find their key. We looked everywhere and in all our things. As a small child I wondered if we would be stuck forever outside our home. My parents' scurrying about made me a bit uneasy. I recall an intense conversation about our dilemma.

After much debate my parents decided to break a small pane of the basement window, and I would crawl in and hurry upstairs to unlock the front door. That was exciting. No, that was a bit scary, because I would have to drop down into a dark basement and find my way to the stairs and then up to the hall. From there it seemed easy to get to the front door. After all, I was a "big" girl. Why was I given this assignment instead of my older brother or even one of my parents? I was the smallest, of course. I was the only one who could fit through the small basement window.

I'm not sure whether that was the first time in my life I was glad I was small. It seems that in your childhood, when you are the youngest and the littlest, you always want to be bigger and older. Here I had the privilege of being the smallest and with that privilege came the responsibility of getting my family back into our house. Was I willing to accept the assignment? Was I going to be okay doing this? As the youngest, I eagerly stepped forward to show my family I really could be a "big" girl.

My father broke the window pane to give me clear access. Now it was my turn. He helped me down into the cellar well, and we stood there together. He went over the plan again with a few last-minute instructions. The space was small. He helped me squeeze through and get my feet onto the ledge next to the window. The lead frame of the window panel brushed my back. My foot hit the ledge and I was in. I must have stood there for more than a minute, because I remember the anxiety in my father's voice coaxing me to get down and go to the front door. Perhaps I was frozen with the realization that I was now in this big house all by myself in a dark basement. And basements can be scary.

Fortunately, the basement was such familiar terrain that I had little trouble finding the stairs. As I made my way to the top, they creaked as they always did. Wooden stairs have a way of letting you know you are on them, and maybe not alone? That's the scary part. I trembled. I could just make out the darkened door to the hallway looming at the top of the stairs. What was on the other side? Was a boogie man waiting for me? Of course it would only be the hallway, but maybe this time things would be different?

Fortunately for this little girl, no boogie man appeared on the other side of the door. As I went through the door, I heard my parents calling to me. "Go to the front door! Go to the front door!" Of course. Where did they think I was headed? Did they think I didn't know where to find the front door? When I approached it, they must have seen me through the side window, because their call changed to, "Open the door! Open the door!" Did they think I planned to stand there and just stare at them through the window?

In my mind the door was very big and very heavy, and that's how I still remember it. The lock was shiny, waiting to be turned. The doorknob felt huge in my small hand. In a moment I flung open the door. I stood there, framed by the doorway, looking at my family. They grinned and cheered. I felt ten feet tall and enormously clever.

These many years later, I'm reminded that life is scary whether we are four, fourteen, or forty. Since my window entry, I've had numerous scares, far more threatening. Unlike when I was four, I've faced many of those scares alone. But was I really alone in those times? Experience and my faith have taught me that I am not alone. In the darkness of aloneness, I have turned to the One I know is always there. "The Lord is my light and my salvation; whom shall I fear? The Lord is the stronghold of my life; of whom shall I be afraid?" (Psalm 27:1). In the stilling of my heart and listening for comfort, I have found the love of God that helps me through the scary times. Times will be scary, but with faith, less scary. Christ's words at the end of the gospel of Matthew echo within my heart. "For remember I am with you always, to the end of the age" (Matthew 28:20).

What about all those locked doors in our lives? All too often, life seems like a series of locked doors whose keys we have lost. We can't open them and so find ourselves frustrated, standing on the other side.

Why are some doors locked to us? Perhaps those doors are locked so that we have to look beyond ourselves in order to get where we're going. We can become so self-reliant that we often are blinded to the help standing right next to us. Look around. Someone or some situation may be readying itself to unlock a door for you. Reflect on that further; maybe it is God who can unlock a door.

I have come to believe responsibility plays a part in opening doors. How we choose to respond ultimately makes the difference. Choosing to act in love responsibly has the potential to open doors. We can't be responsible for opening all doors, but if we keep our eyes and ears open, God will steer us toward the doors we can help open. Is that not our responsibility?

So, who is standing on the other side of that door you open? Who is there to greet you with a smile or a well done? Maybe you know that person well and you aren't surprised to see him or her standing there. Maybe it is someone you never would have thought could possibly be standing there. Maybe it is someone whom you don't even know. Maybe the voice is familiar, but the face not so. And maybe we need to admit to ourselves that we need help to unlock a door, and that a door was often locked, not because of God, but because of us. We keep the door closed. We keep ourselves from hearing God's voice. But when we put God in our hearts, we are able to find the doorknob and the power to swing open the door. And, just as my family smiled and cheered when I opened the door, God smiles on us and cheers us on.

ELEVEN

The Dress

"God is the strength of my heart and my portion forever."
Psalm 73:26

Running.

With more emphasis on the importance of exercise in today's world, running has become more popular and the choice of exercise for thousands; men and women, the young to the elderly. In track meets, marathons, and low-key 5- and 10-kilometer races, in towns and cities worldwide, running has taken off. All you need is a good pair of running shoes and the desire to get moving. I have been a runner for many years now and find it a necessary part of my life. It restores, renews, and makes whole my mind, body, and spirit. It has become life giving. But maybe this has been the case for me from a very early age.

The last snow finally had melted, and I noticed the grass turning green. The longer afternoons brought warmer sunlight. Outside recess at school became a treat. To run in the spring weather was just plain fun.

This particular spring brought with it a whole new experience for me—my first spring at my new school. That fall I had entered the first grade at the country day school in my new hometown in New Jersey. I experienced a lot of "firsts" that year. I soon learned that spring gym classes were focused on the end-of-the-year field day. From kindergarten to eighth grade everyone prepared. Of course it was a far bigger deal for the older kids, but us little guys looked forward to the field day too. Talk circulated through all the classes. Who would run which race and when? Gym classes afforded us the opportunity to practice the distance we were scheduled to run on field day. And so most every day, we ran the fifty-yard dash. Quite naturally, the excitement grew as the spring wore on.

The big day dawned sunny and warm—the perfect day to be outside running. Because of such a special day, my mother thought I should be dressed appropriately. And to be dressed for a special occasion in the 1950s meant a dress.

I was little. I hadn't participated in a field day before. I respected my mother's decisions. And so we picked out one of my pretty party dresses for the occasion. I loved the dress, a light blue with white organdy over a fluffy full skirt. My sneakers completed the outfit. Perfectly, I thought.

When I arrived at school, I found all my classmates were wearing shorts. They were truly ready for a running race. But by then it was too late; I had on what I had on and that was that.

I waltzed into the classroom showing off my beautiful dress. As I reflect back on my grand entrance, I don't remember being stared at or teased for wearing a dress. Clearly, I was dressed very differently from everyone else, but it didn't seem to matter. My classmates took me as part of the gang ready for the field day and the running races. We sat on our desks and chattered as we waited with great excitement for the field day to begin.

As I see myself sitting there in my first grade classroom in my fluffy dress and everyone else in shorts, I wonder about today's world and today's kids. My outfit just did not seem to matter to my friends. We were all kids caught up in the moment. We were friends filled with anticipation and excitement about the races. In reflection, I ponder how the world and society has changed. Peer pressure creates stress in today's world—far too much. If you are not dressed like everyone else, you are different—and being different is often not a good thing. Differences are frowned upon and wondered at. Which clothes you wear are important to fitting in, to being part of the group, and being part of the group is very important. Critical for many. Too often we can't see beyond the clothes on a person's back. "Clothes make the man, or woman," so the saying goes. I wonder. Maybe, maybe not? Would my dress set me apart and make me less than a good friend, less than a good runner, less than the little girl God had called me to be, or less than Ingrid?

Individuals. God created each of us as individuals. This is one of our greatest gifts. To be your own person, acknowledge your own gifts, and use all this to be the person God has created you to be: this is our call. God doesn't want us to be rubber stamps, to each be alike and dress alike. God, I believe, wants us to live out the life with which He has blessed us. Yes, we should be individuals, but we must also learn to live in community with one another.

And here is the challenge, because this calls for acceptance. Are we accepted for who we are? Are we accepted for all we can be? Are we accepting of others? Or have we let society and people squeeze us into a common mold that may or may not fit our individual being? Clearly, these questions didn't concern me that day, dressed in my fluffy blue dress. As I reflect back, I rejoice in the wonder of that day and the acceptance I felt.

The moment finally arrived when my class marched out onto the field with the rest of the school for the competitions to begin. I was so excited I don't think it even occurred to me at first how different my attire was from everyone else's. I was dressed for a party while everyone else was dressed to run. The excitement must have put that potential worry on the back burner.

Even at a young age I possessed a competitive spirit. I liked to win. I knew I could run fast. I wanted to win my race. Finally, as I stood with all the other kids on the field, the realization of the dress hit me.

What about my dress? All the other kids looked so "professional." Could I keep up with them? Only time would tell. We had to wait a seemingly long time before our race was called. Our class watched enthusiastically as the races went off. All the kids seemed to run well. There were easy winners, very close races, and those stragglers who barely finished. I remember feeling anguish for those kids who came in last.

But amazingly, there were few tears among the kids. The excitement of the running race seemed to be enough to carry their spirits through. Those kids won no ribbons but for some reason they seemed to be okay with that. Our teacher had taught us a lesson as we spent the spring preparing for field day. We understood that not everyone could come in first or win a ribbon. We were encouraged to do our best and try as hard as we could, but if we failed to place first, second, or third, that was okay. Participating in the race is what counted.

As we have all no doubt experienced, part of living is just showing up. Life means entering into the race and using our gifts to squeeze as much out of life as we are able. And if we are not first? Well, not everyone can be first. You know that, and I know that. The joy of the kids running the races and coming in last with smiles on their faces for just having the opportunity to be in the race and be with their friends stays with me. They may have lost, but they had showed up. The joy of the moment was not lost on them, for wrapped into the moment was excitement and pure fun. The spectators cheered loudly, with enthusiasm. On the sidelines we kids cheered for everyone. Each of us had a special friend running in a race. In reflection, those cheers held something precious.

Whether we're children or adults, we may not run life's race out in front. Our family and friends may not run in front. We may, in fact, run in the back. But we can cheer one another on. We're called to be in relationship with others, but sometimes we aren't even in the same race as our friends, who live their own lives in their own ways. That doesn't mean we should stand back and take no notice. We need to make the choice to show up, and show up with our support and cheerleading hats on. Everyone deserves a cheerleader willing to show up in his or her life. That is part of the special thing we call relationship. Ask yourself, "Are you willing to be that cheerleader?"

As I've traveled along my faith journey, I have come to know God as my cheerleader. When I feel like I am dead last in this race of life, I have turned to God to cheer me on and lift my spirit. I may not be able to turn and see God standing there waving pompoms on the sidelines, but I have been able to capture that presence. The psalms cheer me forward: "God is the strength of my heart and my portion forever" (Psalm 73:26). "The Lord is my strength and my shield, in him my heart trusts; so I am helped, and my heart exults" (Psalm 28:7). As we turn to God to cheer us on in life, to whom are we passing along those blessed cheers? Like children cheering each other on in the race, may we also be cheerleaders in the varied relationships we cherish.

At long last we were called to the starting line. Fifty yards—the distance we had been practicing. As I stood at the start, the finish line looked really far away. We giggled and wiggled as we tried to make ready for the start. I'd been placed in the middle of the starting line. I looked left and saw my classmates. I looked right and saw my classmates. I looked over them and saw all those cheering parents watching with great anticipation. The sideline was not lost to me because of the significant crowd of mothers and fathers. All eyes turned to the first graders standing at the starting line.

Was I nervous? Probably not, because the excitement was the stronger of the two emotions. This was my first "official" running race at my school's spring field day. There would be many more, but there I was in my fluffy blue party dress. I bent over into a starting position: left leg forward, knee bent, leaning forward, arms ready to pump, looking down the lane to the finish line with great intent.

"Ready, set, go!" Out of the starting blocks we charged. I got a good start, because I remember very early on I could see my lead over the front pack of kids. I ran as hard as I could. And then I ran as hard as I could some more. As the finish line came closer, I ran as hard as I could even more. At this point I could see that I was in front. I had passed all the girls. I had passed all the boys. I had passed all the kids in their shorts. I had passed them wearing my fluffy blue dress that flew in the wind. Quite a sight.

I finished first and jumped for joy. I had won my first "official" race. What joy I felt. That feeling stays with me over fifty years later: the pure joy of a little girl doing her very best with an ability given her by God, and succeeding.

My mother and I have laughed over the years about how I outran the boys in my party dress. We have laughed about the sight of me in my fluffy blue dress and my bare legs running so fast, leaving all the boys behind. Lots of kids came in first in their running races that day, but this particular blue ribbon remains a cherished treasure for this little girl.

This was a day of firsts and lasts. A good friend was last. I was first. My friend wore shorts. I wore a dress. What a pair we made. I had a ribbon. She had no ribbon. First or last, our friendship did not suffer. When it came right down to it, we were just kids running for the excitement and fun of it. We were friends with a relationship that was far more important than places in a running race. Maybe because we were just kids, in our hearts we had life right. Relationship and joy over ribbons and speed, things of the heart and spirit over the physical stuff of the world.

Body and Mind

When I go out for a run today, on certain days when the conditions are just so, I can be reminded of my fluffy blue dress and a treasured race way back in first grade. I feel comfortable with whatever pace I am able to run now. I feel grateful that I can still run and still want to run. Just as back in the first grade, running is a matter of the spirit, of lessons learned. For me, running is life renewing and life giving and a gift of God.

TWELVE

Music

"Make a joyful noise to the Lord"
Psalm 100:1

God and family have blessed Bill and me with a delightful grandson, Davis. When Davis comes to visit he fills our home with great joy. He rushes to the backdoor and rings the bell to announce his arrival. "Ding, dong." The door swings open and he charges in with a smile. Since his birth three years ago, I have been collecting toys for him to play with when visiting his grandparents. After a quick "hi" he runs for the toy box and begins covering the family room floor with toys. He's a "cause and effect" little guy. He loves to push a button and watch what happens. So I've gathered an assortment of playthings that hum, vibrate, rattle, and play music. At times Davis tries to activate all of these toys simultaneously; he rushes from toy to toy to keep the action going.

Our piano in the living room gives him great pleasure. Again, cause and effect. Davis climbs up on the piano seat and taps the spot next to him, indicating where I should sit. Then our concert begins. With great precision he moves his little fingers across the black and white keys, picking out one note at a time. Then there is a crash of thunder as he hits the keys in the lower range with both hands. We laugh at the created thunder. Then I play the higher notes very softly and quickly to give the impression of rain. Thunder and then rain. We're quite the duo. Often when I sit with Davis at the piano, making noises of expression, I reflect back on the days when I took piano lessons and on my life's musical career, which has been varied and often not successful.

Dancing has been part of that journey. Why would anyone want to stand on their toes? It looks so painful. But that was my goal when I took ballet lessons as a young girl. Like so many other little girls, I loved getting all dressed up in a tutu. The ones with the flaring crinoline skirts were the best. My ballet grand finale took place before I entered junior high. My ballet class had learned to dance in toe shoes. Mine were pink with hard toes and with pink satin ribbon that I laced around my ankles and legs to keep the shoes in place. To make standing on my toes as comfortable as possible, I stuffed lamb's wool into the shoes. I felt like a prima ballerina.

Our recital number was named "Falling Leaves." We ballerinas wore dark green leotards with small softly flowing skirts. But the best part was the leaves that our mothers sewed onto the front of the leotard. From shoulder to waist we had three-dimensional leaves in autumn reds, yellows, and bronzes. Our routine required that we float across the stage in a line, on our toes. Our arms reached gracefully upward and moved rhythmically up and down, creating the effect of falling leaves. Circling, we toed from stage right to stage left. The piano's tinkling created the impression of rain and falling leaves. My friends and I thought we were graceful and gorgeous. Our families told us so. But I wonder. Fifty years later, my mother and I still laugh about "Falling Leaves" and the pain of skittering across a stage on in toe shoes. Charming, but probably not graceful.

Through my elementary school years, I tried my hand at different musical instruments. First, I decided to learn to play the violin. I can't remember why, but my parents indulged me. They arranged for a violin and a class for me. What a struggle from day one of a very short career as a violinist. I had trouble holding the bow and reading the music, but the real problem was I could not tune the violin. My teacher always asked how I could play such a fine instrument when it was so out of tune. He'd tune it and play for me. "See how beautiful it sounds?" he'd say. Years later, my mother would tell me that my teacher kept me as his student only, because he loved to play my violin. Within a year I realized that I was tone deaf. I just couldn't hear the notes. I could not hear the difference between the notes. Therefore, I could never tune my violin. And so I moved on to the piano.

I felt I had half a chance with the piano, because I didn't have to tune it. I just had to read music and move my fingers delicately and precisely over the keys. My teacher, Mrs. Macarthy, lived in a creepy old house, but she was understanding and had a good way with kids. I practiced every morning before I went to school and every afternoon before I did my homework. I liked playing the piano. I believe I even got pretty good.

As I reflect back on my career as a pianist, I remember a particular piece. For the final spring piano recital one year, I played a piece with four other students. "In a Persian Market" was written for three pianos. At each of two pianos, one person plays the treble part while the other plays the bass. A single pianist plays the third piano, between the other two. All spring, each of us in the quintet practiced our individual parts separately. I learned to play the bass part for one of the duets. It was a bit strange to play notes that conveyed a rhythm but no melody.

A couple of weeks before the big day, I joined my friend, Sandy, who had learned the treble part of the piece that accompanied my bass. We practiced together. With four hands working in sync, the music and melody came alive. I thought, "This sounds really good." When the four of us who had learned the duet parts and the soloist felt ready, we all played together. That first practice was a nightmare. We were ahead of each other and then behind one another. This was a lot tougher than I'd thought. Finally, we were sufficiently coordinated that Mrs. Macarthy felt we could perform reasonably well in the recital.

Parents filled the huge living room of Mrs. Macarthy's house. The three pianos stood stately at one end. The five pianists appeared from the next room, and a dead silence engulfed the room. We sat down and readied ourselves. On cue from Mrs. Macarthy, we began. Magically, we all started together. As we played on, the piece came alive for the audience. My left hand fingers failed me a couple of times. We all missed a note here and there and knew it. But we kept playing. Today as I hear the piece in my memory, I remember it was quite spectacular to hear three pianos being played simultaneously. After the last note was hit with perfect timing, the five of us stood, faced the audience, and bowed. Sandy and I beamed at each other—quite the duo of the quintet.

With such success behind me, I continued to take piano lessons when I went to high school. Perhaps the musical world was doable after all. However, all first-year students were required to take music appreciation. Piano, yes, music appreciation I wasn't so sure about. In the end, this class cured me of all musical instrument ambition. One of the first weeks of class the teacher, Mr. Enmon, wanted all of us to sing the scale: "Do re mi fa so la ti do." The first two girls sang it easily and sounded good. Mr. Enmon turned to me: "It's your turn." Sinking low in my seat, I boldly told him I didn't want to do it, because I knew I couldn't sing. He insisted.

"No. I can't sing."

"Of course everyone can sing. Besides, this is just a high school classroom."

"No." But I had to. "Do re mi..."

"That's enough. You're right; you can't sing." Never again was I asked to sing in that class or any other.

By the time I was a teenager, I knew which gifts were mine and which were definitely not mine. I've grown to appreciate the blessings of differing gifts from God. I more fully understand, "there are varieties of gifts, but the same Spirit; and there are varieties of services, but the same Lord; and there are varieties of activities, but it is the same God who activates all of them in everyone. To each is given the manifestation of the Spirit for the common good" (1 Corinthians 12.4–7). Discovering our gifts opens our life to a fuller meaning. I believe God calls us to use our gifts in service to others and to better our own lives. Through athletics I've known successes and a healthier life. For that I give thanks. I know I lack the gift of carrying a tune. That gift was not mine to receive. But that realization has given me the freedom to enjoy music in my own way, a freedom that has kept me dancing.

In high school and college, my dancing moved into the rock 'n' roll of the '60s. The music of those years fed my spirit. Any opportunity I had to party and dance, I joined in. My last year of high school, my Uncle Erik threw a memorably outrageous party for older teens and a handful of parents, family, and friends. He hired a band called the Basement Wall and, ironically, rented the basement room in a hotel. The room was hardly big enough. Crowded on the dance floor, we bumped elbows, hips, and bottoms. The Basement Wall was fantastic. They had us dancing all night. The adults had as much fun as the teenagers, if not more. Teens danced with adults. Everyone danced with everyone in circles. The music was so great that we got up and danced even if we didn't have a partner. The music went on for hours. Celebration and joy filled the room and everyone's heart and spirit. Young and old had good plain fun. The music electrified the night.

To dance, to live, to love. From the night of rock 'n' roll I fast-forward to another occasion on which dance touched hearts in a special way. I was in my early twenties and dressed all in white except for a small blue bow sewn onto the hem of my dress. My head was covered with the most beautiful veil that fell down my back; the lace around its edge matched the lace of my dress. An hour before, I had stood at my church's altar and held the hands of my husband-to-be. In the evening light, we had exchanged vows. Now the evening's music was celebrating love and a new path for our lives.

As my husband escorted me on to the dance floor that night, I was on cloud nine. When we reached the middle of the floor, we turned and embraced each other with a smile. With one hand, Bill gently touched my back; with the other, he held my hand. Neither of us really knew how to ballroom dance, so he gently guided me around the floor. It was a rhythm of love and a new life. I treasured that music and first dance as a married woman. Friends and family applauded enthusiastically, and I felt like this dreamland held us in a magical moment.

These many years later, I still have on tape the ceremony and music from our wedding. When I listened to this tape for the first time in over thirty years, my eyes filled with tears. I was in my car and had to pull over and stop to listen more closely and dry my eyes.

Jesus' first miracle occurred at a wedding that he, his mother, and his disciples attended. The wedding, in Cana, was far from over when the host ran out of wine. Without enough wine for his guests, the host would suffer embarrassment and a stain on his family's reputation. Jesus instructed the servants to bring him barrels of water. He then turned the water into wine. The host declared this wine better than the wine he'd been serving, and his guests praised him for saving the best wine for last. In this story Jesus, the man, became real to me and human. Like most of us, Jesus enjoyed a good party and wanted the very best for the host. When I think about the many parties I have attended in my lifetime and what a good time I have had, I reflect that people of all ages love parties. We love music and to dance.

Recently, Bill and I had one of our most delightful musical experiences. We took lessons on Sunday afternoons in swing dancing. We both have two left feet, but we thought it might be fun. We might even learn how to do fast dances, so we could enjoy more readily the weddings and parties we attended. The classroom was a small dance studio with one wall entirely a mirror. There were four other couples. I think we were all a bit nervous as we started out, especially when we learned we'd have to switch partners. Stepping on your spouse's feet was one thing; stepping on a stranger's is quite another. Our teacher gently led us through the basic steps. Carefully and intentionally we moved around the floor, all the time viewing our movements in the mirror. Bill and I made some progress that first lesson.

By the third week we were gaining confidence and moving with greater ease. The beat became easier to pick up, and we progressed from self-consciousness to experiencing the dance. I actually enjoyed switching partners and learning to follow another man. We laughed at our mistakes, our stepping on toes, or missing the underarm swing. As the weeks passed, the moves became more difficult. Bill and I kept up. Those Sunday afternoons on the dance floor became a real treat. We had successfully ventured down a new musical path. We weren't great, and we'll never be great, but I gave thanks for the joy of the moment.

The spring after those classes we attended our niece's wedding and Bill received a great compliment: our daughter, Christina, asked him to teach her how to swing. They weren't bad. A bit sloppy but having a great time. Swinging with my husband was a whole new experience for us.

I have great respect for the musically gifted. I love a beautiful voice, jazz played on a piano, a rhythm played on a guitar. I know I can't sing, but that is one reason I go to church. My grandmother used to tell me that you go to church as a youngster to learn the words to the hymns so that when you're old and you can no longer read the words in the hymnal, you still can sing the hymns. My eyesight has yet to fail, but singing hymns in church satisfies my hunger to sing. I sing my heart out in worship, and it makes no difference whether or not I'm on key.

I believe God loves any voice raised in joyful praise. To sing before the Lord with all my heart and soul feeds my faith journey. Singing while standing in front of my friend Bob is an added treat. Bob also loves to sing, but he always sings off-key, too. I'm sure if the music was played more softly we would sound like two howling wolves on a full moonlit night. No matter. Our hearts are tuned in to praise and worship. God loves a singing heart.

Organ notes float forth from pipes with a familiar hymn. Or a band strikes up an upbeat tune. For even the most musically untalented among us, to dance, to sing is to praise a God of unconditional love. "Make a joyful noise to the Lord, all the earth. Worship the Lord with gladness; come into his presence with singing" (Psalm 100:1–2).

THIRTEEN

The War

"To God the things that are God's"
Mark 12:17

Tall, stately eucalyptus trees marked the California campus with an aura of peacefulness and history, due to their size and age. They symbolized life at college for me for my first three years. And then life turned upside down. The world around us, as we had known it, began to crumble around us in the fourth year. For the first time in my lifetime, people I knew were going off to war and were dying there. The Vietnam War was quietly slicing up my life into emotions I had never had to contend with before.

Walking alone across campus in the morning's first light, for an eight o'clock class, gave me time to wake up and prepare for the day ahead. I came to appreciate those few moments of solitude. The damp fog had yet to burn off. Mist veiled my path and the lush vegetation. I was happy that the morning trek led downhill from my apartment. It seemed easier to be walking *down* at that hour and not having to trudge *up*. I walked past the music center and down the main street toward the classroom building. At the Student Union I stopped to study the sculpture, created by students, on the front steps. What was this really all about? I asked myself. A gigantic Band-Aid standing on its side. Its creators had hinged together three door-size panels, painted them pink, and pierced the central "pad" with air holes. The word *healing* appeared across the Band-Aid in large artsy lettering.

Our world was indeed in need of healing. We were bleeding both literally and figuratively. Young men and women headed to Vietnam to fight a war that struck at the very heart of us students. What could we do? I believe, in our powerlessness, we felt the need to protest. Protests rang out from college campuses across the country. What a tragic event at Kent State University. Members of my generation won't easily forget the photo of a young woman kneeling over a slain fellow student, her face expressing horror. The protests at my college were relatively sedate. But standing in front of the Band-Aid, I knew that healing for us, our country, and our world, would be a long time coming.

Thinking about the Vietnam War and the political chaos growing in our country, I hurried on to class. I caught up to a friend, and we walked together. After exchanging a casual, "good morning," we walked in silence. What was there to talk about? At times I was almost afraid to begin a conversation for fear of where it would lead. The war seemed to consume our thoughts, often pushing our studies to the back burner. This was difficult for me, because I was just weeks away from graduation. I had spent four years working hard to do well in college. I had invested many hours in my education, and it felt like all that was now slipping away. My friend opened the conversation with comments about a newspaper article about the war. We walked, she talked, and I didn't say anything. In her ranting she gave me little opportunity to speak, and I was secretly glad for it.

All this protest stuff exhausted me. The painful emotions which arose within me, I had never known before. There were young men fighting in the jungles of a country halfway around the world. They had been called to serve their country, and many did, and many died. One of those young men was my brother. He had received orders to do his tour of duty in Vietnam. I felt that I would betray him if I decried the war. I was scared he would not return, but a lot of other families were worried about their loved ones, also. Everyone knew someone connected to the fighting and dying. You couldn't get away from it. I was glad when we reached the classroom and my friend's tirade ended.

During the week, my friends and I struggled to accomplish our class work amid an atmosphere of anger and protest. Then we decided to get away. We all knew of San Francisco's Haight-Ashbury district and its counterculture of hippies, free love, and drugs. A short drive over the Bay Bridge brought us there. Partly because I was an athlete, I had no interest in taking drugs, but I watched stoned people. They appeared to be lost in space and time. I supposed that was one way to cope with world events: tune out. The street was packed with long-haired hippies in tie-dyed shirts and leather pants and sandals. The shops featured incense, psychedelic posters, and earrings that hung to the shoulders. I felt that if I bought something I'd be connected to current fads without falling, like many of my friends, into the abyss of drugs and free love. I'd participate, but safely.

As the weeks ticked by and spring moved toward summer, I learned that my brother had finished his tour of duty in Vietnam and was headed home. We were one of the lucky families. Brother, husband, son unharmed on his way home. He was to arrive in Oakland when he landed in the States. I received a call from my parents requesting that I pick him up. Would I pick him up? Of course I would pick him up. I don't know if my brother, even to this day, knows what excitement and how privileged I felt being the first to welcome him home to the States. The hours seemed longer in those days as I awaited his arrival. But the day did finally arrive. As I drove over to the army base, I remember trembling. What would he look like? What would be the first words between us?

There he was! An extremely handsome young man in uniform, walking toward me. I hadn't seen my brother in his uniform before. He walked tall, with a bounce in his step. There must have been other soldiers around, but I saw only him. Was this the brother with whom I'd so often played, argued, fought, and laughed as a child? In the flesh, it was. Seeing him for the first time after so many months away at war. How did it make me feel? To put that into words is very difficult. It's just there, a priceless and timeless resident within my mind, heart, and soul.

That night he treated me to dinner at a fine San Francisco restaurant. He ordered a steak with all the trimmings. I thought how long it must have been since he'd enjoyed such a meal. During dinner he regaled me with his tales from the war. It was unreal, but real. Too real sometimes. The stories of a foreign land touched me through this person I loved, and I was truly happy, glad, elated—perhaps all these—to be sitting next to him. One story in particular has remained with me throughout the more than thirty years that have passed. I am positive its impact has been far greater on him than me, but that is true for so many of my generation who live with the memories of the Vietnam War.

My brother and another soldier were traveling by jeep through the Vietnamese countryside. Based on a current security briefing, they had been advised not to stop until they reached their destination. My brother was driving as they entered a small village and drove down its main dirt road. Out of the corner of his eye, he noticed a group of children playing by the roadside. Suddenly a boy on a bike came out of nowhere and rode right in front of the jeep. In that fraction of a second the jeep struck and went over the child. Even though he had been advised not to stop, realizing what had happened, my brother stopped the jeep, got out, and hurried back to the boy, who lay in the dirt road. Villagers began gathering around to see what had happened. The tension in the air could have been cut with a knife.

My brother remembered the security briefing, but he couldn't just leave this child lying there. He knelt down and picked up the injured boy. His only thoughts were of the child who had been an innocent victim of a war. Surrounded by men, women, and children, he carried the child, limp in his arms, to the nearest hut. His only thought was to get the boy out of the road and into shelter. Still surrounded by villagers, he gently laid the boy down. What happened next was almost unbelievable. My brother said that someone was truly looking over him that day, because incredibly, a U.S. patrol with a medic happened to arrive. As the medic began attending to the boy, he quietly told my brother to leave as inconspicuously as possible. My brother backed away, returned to his jeep, and slowly drove away.

This did not win or lose the war, but for me it remains in my heart as an example of how one human being can and will care for another even as a war rages around them. No great rescue of a patrol or soldier. No dodging of bullets or bombs or running for cover. No helicopters fell from the sky or great plumes of smoke rose from the jungle. This incident would never make the evening news or be depicted in any great movie. Blessedly though, it was one life of one child who was not left to die in a war, because someone could not leave that little life to die.

I remember my brother as he told this story over dinner that night more than thirty years ago. I could see into his heart. I could see a soldier who fought in a war, because he was called to do so. But this soldier did it with the highest value being placed on life and liberty. As I reflect on this Vietnam incident, I hear the words of Scripture: "Jesus said to them, 'Give to the emperor the things that are the emperor's, and to God the things that are God's.' And they were utterly amazed at him" (Mark 12:17). A war is of the emperor's, but a life is of God. To serve your country for freedom and justice is a call from the emperor; to show mercy and compassion for a child's life is from God.

It is so easy to forget how precious life is. I take it for granted too many times. The minutes slip through my hands and are gone before I know it. A breath comes and goes in a moment, and I forget how it keeps me alive. I take a step or run a mile with the presumption that this is how it is supposed to be. That this is my privilege when in fact it is really a gift from God. What is the life of a child of "the enemy" worth? I suspect for many it would have been just another casualty of war. For my brother that life had meaning. He could not just walk away. Through all the killing of the Vietnam era and the many lives maimed and lost, I treasure this one incident as an example of respecting the gift of life. And so, in war lives are saved as well as taken. The Band-Aid in front of my college's Student Union protested the taking of life. Healing needed to happen, but at that time we all wondered if it would happen and when. As I look around at today's world, I am wondering the same thing. Healing needs to happen. I often reflect on the lessons of healing that could have been learned from the Vietnam era and wonder what was learned. Anything at all?

During the time of the Vietnam War many believed God was dead. How could God be alive in such a time of violence and killing, of death and war? The Vietnam War was a different kind of war from the great wars of the generations before when soldiers fought for freedom, their country standing behind them with national pride. I was of the generation that saw no reason for the killing of our brothers, sisters, and friends in a part of the world that seemed so irrelevant to us. Was God dead? How could that be, though, if there were men and women who believed and acted as my brother did? Through my spiritual journey I have come to believe that God was not dead, but He was crying copious tears. How could God not shed tears over a situation tearing apart the world He had created? I believe God was, and is, there always. It is we who turn away, and then profess that God is dead. I have only to remember those who saved a life in the war and see God at work in the hearts of God's people, in their own quiet way amid all the turmoil. God is there. Where are we?

The night of our reunion dinner, my brother stayed in my apartment. The next morning we shared breakfast. Then he changed into his uniform. When he emerged from the bedroom, he made a request of me that I will never forget. He wanted his uniform to look neat and pressed, but his shirt was much too large. Would I, he asked, take a tuck in the back of his shirt? He turned his back to me. For the first time, I noticed how much extra material there was in his shirt. I took a huge tuck so that his shirt lay flat across his chest. "Did this shirt used to fit?" I asked.

"It was a little big when I left for Vietnam."

"Really? Only a little?"

The toll of war came home to me. My brother was well. One of the lucky ones. He hadn't been disabled or killed. But even he had been physically diminished. I was struck by his weight loss. The tuck I made represented all that he'd endured, and escaped. In ways sometimes not obvious, war ravages even healthy men and women, left seemingly intact. I was moved in a way that escapes words. Its only explanation lay in the reality of a situation that would bring me to reflection and thanksgiving over the years to follow.

After taking my brother to the airport, I found myself once more in the presence of the Band-Aid sculpture. Its meaning hung over me as I made my way to class. I was one of many to take a stand on the issues of the Vietnam War. Many of my friends chose to protest by marching and creating images of protest, such as this huge Band-Aid. As graduation approached, the academic dean suspended the last week of classes and final exams became optional. The college and students talked about canceling our graduation ceremony. Many colleges went this route. I lobbied against this at mine. I had worked hard for four years, really hard for four years, to get my college degree. Perhaps it was selfish, but I wanted the college to recognize me for my work and studies. I took a stand for graduation, not protest. Clearly I was in the minority, but I did what I thought was the right thing to do. I saw nothing to be gained by canceling graduation as a protest to the war. The Vietnam War was ruining enough lives. Would it even ruin the lives of those of us who were trying to carry on with life at home? I took my final exams, and, with pride in a job well done, I marched into my graduation with my fellow classmates, many of whom were adorned with symbols of protest for the war and many with symbols for peace.

But the questions still remain. When will unjust wars be over? How many more lives will be lost in combat? When will our world know peace?

FOURTEEN

The Ambulance

"He will wipe every tear from their eyes."
Revelation 21:3–4

Like most mornings for mothers with young children, that morning was hectic. I was running around getting Jonathan and Brooks ready for school. Everyone had eaten breakfast. I'd put the dishes into the dishwasher, and I'd made last-minute adjustments to the boys' outfits.

Upstairs brushing my teeth, I could hear the boys fooling around very loudly downstairs. I thought, "I've got to get down there before things get out of control." At the top of the stairs I made a fast turn around the banister and started down. At the third step, my running shoe got caught on the rug and sent me tumbling. As I rolled down the first flight of stairs, I felt a sharp pain in my left ankle. I hit the wall directly in front of me. The collision kept me from careening down the rest of the stairs. I lay for a moment in a crumpled ball, half-dazed. When I realized what had happened, I cursed my carelessness. The pain in my ankle was so severe I feared that if I tried to get up I might pass out. Having heard the thud, Jonathan came running. He stood at the bottom of the stairs looking up at me in disbelief.

"Call 911, call 911," I managed to get out. "Tell them Mommy has just fallen down the stairs. Tell them to come quickly." I heard Jonathan make the call from the kitchen phone and gave thanks for his calmness. He reported back that the police and ambulance were on the way. Thinking it best not to move, I just lay there. The boys stood at the bottom of the stairs staring up at me with blank expressions. A short time later, which seemed forever, the police and then the Emergency Medical Technicians (EMTs) were in the house. My sons moved aside as the team immediately began work on me.

As the EMTs were checking my vital signs and getting a report on the accident, the phone rang. I heard the police chief answer the phone. Bill was calling and, needless to say, he was taken back when he heard the chief answering his home phone at seven thirty in the morning. In that instant his imagination went wild. What in heaven's name was the police chief doing in his house? He was relieved to hear that I had only fallen down the stairs. "Not to worry, Bill," the police chief said. "We've got everything under control here."

I was packaged onto the ambulance gurney and taken off to the local hospital. A friend took my youngest son to nursery school, and the chief gave Jonathan a ride to school in his cruiser. Jonathan thought this adventure was "cool." That morning was the beginning of a new life's journey for me.

A year later Dover's fire department put out an appeal for new EMTs. They were putting together a class of interested people. When I read an article about this in the local newspaper, I remembered my experience with the ambulance and its personnel when I had fallen down the stairs. They'd been wonderful. I immediately wanted to give back to the town for all they had done for me. After careful consideration and a heartfelt discussion with my family, I registered for the EMT class. We students, twenty-four men and women of different ages, quickly bonded in our intense study to become medical professionals. Night meeting upon night meeting, textbook page after page, we grew in knowledge and experience in how to react and treat people in emergency medical situations. As the weeks unfolded we all gained confidence, which created a certain passion for wanting to help those in urgent need.

After eight months of book study and training, we all passed the state EMT exam and were certified. That was an amazing class for me. The wealth of knowledge I gained from that study now humbles me. How did I manage to learn so much in such a short time while taking care of four children and a husband? When I completed the class' final exam, I felt ready to respond to any ambulance call. I was eager to get started.

Over the years that I served the fire department as an on-call EMT, I dealt with situations ranging from insignificant to life-threatening. For example, we gave an elderly woman a ride to the emergency room simply so she could be checked by her doctor, but I also crawled into the back seat of a smashed car and held traction on the driver's neck to prevent paralysis. Every incident was unique. Every injured person required me to give of myself. I carry with me a number of ambulance runs that ended in great sadness and others that ended in pure joy.

It was midmorning when my EMT beeper sounded its tone. Over the transmitter the police gave the location of the 911 call. This emergency was right down the street from my home. I knew the ambulance would be coming from the center of town staffed with EMTs on board, so I headed directly to the scene of the emergency. When I reached the address and turned in the driveway, I realized that I knew this family. On a 911 call, such a situation can be difficult. Knowing the person who is lying in the bed or trapped in the car can elicit emotions that get tangled in one's medical work.

When I pulled up to the house, a police car was already parked in the driveway. I called out as I entered the house. Someone called back from the far end of the first floor. I made my way down the hall and found the bedroom where the family and police were gathered. Jed's elderly mother lay in the bed. Deathly pale, she didn't move and was unresponsive. Pain and panic were written all over the faces of her family.

On my heels came the rest of the EMTs off the ambulance, and we quickly assessed the situation. No pulse. No breathing. Her heart had stopped, and so two EMTs started CPR while a member of our team obtained the patient's history and what had happened. Her son Jed was the clearest about the morning's events. Time was of the essence. We EMTs worked quickly and efficiently as a team to save her life. All our training and experience were called into play.

While continuing CPR we placed the elderly woman on the ambulance gurney and started out of the house. As we rolled down the hall, we counted the chest compressions and the number of the breaths given. An EMT checked her pulse. Still no response. We continued with aggressive CPR. In the driveway, just as we were about to load the elderly woman into the ambulance, Jed said,

"You know, there is a 'do not resuscitate' order on my mother." No, we hadn't known that. Somewhere in her room, words on a piece of paper declared that death should be allowed to occur under dire circumstances. And so in the next few moments an emotional and medical dilemma unfolded.

Protocol states that once an EMT has begun CPR in the field they must continue until the patient is delivered to personnel with more advanced training. However, given the existence of a "do not resuscitate" order, we should not have started CPR. Such an order is obviously serious and usually final. It conveys the patient's wishes and indicates that the matter was carefully considered. So those of us on the ambulance that day found ourselves in both a professional and heart-wrenching dilemma.

Jimmy, the lead EMT, told Jed that we shouldn't continue CPR, because doing so would violate his mother's expressed wishes. Jed cringed. "Don't let her go. Don't let her go," he sobbed. But his mother's instructions had clearly indicated that she did not want aggressive CPR. We knew we were legally obligated to continue, but still we could not dismiss the verbal request of the son. We looked into the pain of Jed's face and heard the huge sadness in his voice. Our exchange with him continued as we moved closer to the ambulance. "Okay. Okay. Stop the CPR," Jed said with anguish. "No. No. Keep going. I don't want her to die!" These words were extremely painful for us. We knew what we should do professionally, but the son's distress couldn't be ignored. The situation became more emotionally difficult, because by the time we reached the ambulance we knew we probably could not save her life. We had a pulse, but that was only from the CPR. Her color remained ashen white, and she showed no sign of life. Even with those signs, the reality was that a precious life still lay before us. A mother who was loved dearly by a son.

Those few moments have etched themselves into my mind and heart. I witnessed the powerful pain of letting go of a loved one. Split-second decisions pulled at the very being of who we all were. The sadness of reality grabbed us. For me, that sadness seemed to say: *don't you ever forget this, don't you ever forget these faces.* We couldn't save her. But how could we let death have the last word with so much effort pouring forth and her son begging us not to lose her?

As we loaded Jed's mother into the ambulance, we EMTs made a decision. We would continue CPR to the hospital, because of our legal obligation, but less aggressively, and we would not resuscitate her any further. As we pulled away from the house, I watched Jed get into his car to follow us to the hospital. The pain all over his face, and eyes filled with tears, told the story.

Under such circumstances death is gut-wrenching. As I reflect on that ambulance run, and again feel the grief, I turn to my faith seeking comfort for Jed and myself. "And I heard a loud voice from the throne saying, 'See, the home of God is among mortals. He will dwell with them; they will be his peoples, and God himself will be with them; he will wipe every tear from their eyes. Death will be no more; mourning and crying and pain will be no more, for the first things have passed away' " (Revelation 21:3–4). Death's power can be indescribable. It's written, in grief, all over the faces of those left behind. I believe that God shares the pain of death with everyone it touches. And through His grace, God makes it less painful. God grieves for the loved ones and with the loved ones. He will wipe every tear from their eyes.

After such a difficult ambulance run, we EMTs would gather to debrief. Later that morning, those of us who had been on the call to Jed's house sat in a circle looking into each other's eyes. We talked about what we had done professionally, the good parts and the less than good parts. We analyzed and re-analyzed the situation and the facts. We encouraged each other to consider the decisions we'd made and commented on some of those things that needed to be improved. Most of all, we reached out to one another and gave one another permission to feel all the emotions running through us. I felt relieved. It was very cathartic for me to know that I wasn't alone in my grief or in the frustration I felt being powerlessness in the face of death. All the training in the world would not have saved that woman's life. We knew that, but the pain remained.

My work as an EMT brought sadness, but it yielded great joy, too. The small child was choking horribly when we went through the door. Ashen-faced and with a look of desperation, his mother held him in her arms. My colleague, Billy, grabbed the child, turned him over his arm, and firmly patted his back. Nothing. Billy patted again. Nothing. A third time. Nothing. The fourth time, a carrot flew from the child's mouth, and he started to cry. He turned pink as the tears ran down his face. His mother, too, was weeping, but her tears were tears of pure joy. As we rode to the hospital to get the child checked out, the mother sat close to him, rubbing his hair and speaking to him softly to keep him calm. The love between mother and son overflowed onto us EMTs riding in the back of the ambulance, filling our hearts with happiness and relief.

But perhaps my greatest joy on an ambulance run came on another call. The police dispatched the ambulance to a home where the call had come from the husband, "She's going to have the baby, right now. Help." When the ambulance squad arrived, we found the wife lying on the bathroom floor panting and sweating. She managed to say, "He's coming. He's coming." A contraction hit and she squelched the scream. Our EMT named Catherine was first on the floor next to her. With a quick inspection, she could see the baby's head crowning. Three of us EMTs crowded into this small bathroom to attend to the mother and baby. Within moments the baby was in Catherine's hands, crying. Elation shone from the mother's face, which was encircled by her hair dripping with perspiration. We EMTs, too, were thrilled and filled with satisfaction.

A life is very real and fragile for an Emergency Medical Technician. I and my fellow EMTs experienced death and life—the pain of loss and the joy of rescue. I pause to remember and give thanks for the people I worked with all those years. They were so professional: well trained, well equipped, highly skilled, in some cases truly gifted. I could name their skills, but it went deeper than that. Importantly, they had an inner sense of how to deal with people, pain and grief, as well as those moments of joy. In the end we worked together. We were only human beings doing all that was humanly possible to save lives, given the circumstances.

The baby we delivered bears the name of one of the EMTs. The son who lost his mother asked me to conduct his own memorial service when the time came.

FIFTEEN

The Race

"For God's temple is holy, and you are that temple."
1 Corinthians 3:17

Thousands assembled. Each person an individual. Each person a part of this mass of humanity waiting to start. The runners jumped, stretched, and jogged in place. Each had their own way of staying warm, releasing stored energy, and coping with the excitement. Every runner had a story to tell about how they'd reached the starting line of the Boston Marathon. Mine was probably no different than many, and yet at the same time it was unique to me and my life circumstances.

I was forty-four years old, and running was part of my very being. Every day I followed a carefully laid-out schedule of workouts. My goal: to run in the Boston Marathon. I knew that over the years many runners had jumped into this race at the end of the pack to run with "the runners." My goal: to be one of "the runners" who had qualified for the marathon, therefore earning an official race number. My workouts became as difficult as they were exhilarating, with a vein of toughness in mind and persevering spirit running throughout them. When your legs ache, your toes hurt, and you wonder if you can draw another breath, your spirit carries you forward. I was training my body and spirit for the run of my life.

The nine months of training before the marathon had been good. The New England weather had not been terribly cold and without excessive snow to clog the roads. I stayed healthy through the winter. Workouts went well and according to schedule. I finally reached a point in my training when I was confident I could cover the distance if I could keep my body injury free. My mantra became: stay with the routine, pay attention to what your body is saying, and keep the finish line at the forefront. I would be ready.

As I stood at the starting line, the finish line in Boston flashed across my mind's eye. It was more real in that moment than it had ever been. It was going to be a very long way, but a sense of confidence spread over me. Because of my high race number, I was way back in the pack of runners. A sea of runners stretched out before me. No way could I see the starting line, but I would get there soon enough. The day was cool, but the forecast predicted greater warmth as the day progressed. An old pair of socks covered my hands, which not only served to keep my hands warm, but also my arms. My strategy was to throw off the socks to some youngster along the route when the chill had left my body.

The general pack of runners lined up well before the starting gun was to go off. Those twenty to thirty minutes seemed like an eternity. Anxiety and excitement saturated the pack of runners. You would have been numb not to feel it. Here I was after many years of running and nine months of hard work. I was ready to go. Boy, was I ready to go. I was prepared to make this incredible journey of 26.2 miles to Boston with all these runners.

Although I didn't hear the starting gun, my watch showed twelve noon so I knew it must have gone off. We slowly inched forward. I took in the surrounding faces. Men with unshaven faces. Women with confidence written in their eyes. Older people and younger people shining with smiles and laughter. An occasional intense stare pierced the crowd. Many chatted with their friend or the stranger who happened to be standing beside them. All eyes were forward, forward to the actual starting line painted on the pavement ahead. We walked a few steps, jogged a few, waited a minute or two for the crowd to move forward again. The excitement filled every one of my muscles from face to feet. The starting line, there it was at last. I crossed it, started my running watch, and the race of my life had begun.

Because of all the runners around and ahead of me, the pace going down the hill away from the starting line was slow. I reminded myself to be patient. I had a long way to go, and there was nothing to be gained by running around people, other than very sore hips from excessive movement sideways instead of forward. With each step, I intentionally took in everything happening in front and to the sides of me.

I thought, *how often do we "run" through life and not look around us. Are we too busy with schedules and things that need to get done that we miss the small things?* I was not going to do that at this time and in this place because I knew I would never pass this way again. The running shirts and hats, the crowd on the side of the road, the faces and chatter, became a play on a stage. I took my place within all of this. My legs were fresh and my spirit revved up, so it was easy to pay attention to all these little things. A smile passed over my face: *I'm here and I'm really doing this. Enjoy this moment, because it will not be so easy farther down the road.*

After the second mile or so, the runners around me began to thin out. I started to run at my own pace. I fell in with a group of runners going my speed. It felt good to be in sync with this company of runners. The company felt strangely good, the finest company for this time in my life. I was where I wanted to be, doing what I wanted to do. I was enthralled not only by the runners, but by all the spectators lining the road cheering for us. An occasional voice could be heard yelling words of encouragement. It was tempting to say: *save those words for later, it's going to be a whole lot more difficult at mile twenty than mile two.* There were thousands of us running by and yet each cheer felt like it was just for me. Or, at the very least, I took in each cheer as an encouragement for my individual effort in this long run.

Town after town passed by. The sun had come out, and the temperature was rising. The socks on my hands were long gone. A couple of miles back, I had thrown them to a little boy with outstretched hands. As I purposefully threw them to him, he smiled at his trophy. It tickled me to think that someone actually thought my old socks were worth something. But then again, it was a real-life souvenir from the Boston Marathon. Did that make me special?

With each passing mile I became increasingly conscious of my body's need for water. I was not particularly thirsty at that point, but I knew that if I didn't drink now I would pay the price later. At a water station, I ran over and grabbed a paper cup of water. Ever tried drinking and running at the same time? It is not easy. To avoid spilling too much, I squeezed the cup to a narrow spout that directed the water into my mouth. Having run road races before, I'd gotten pretty good at this technique. I knew that my body would be craving liquid by the end of the race. The goal now was to stay as hydrated as possible. As a runner, I had learned how important water is to the body.

By the time I reached the halfway point, I was hot. The sun had been beating down on me for almost two hours. I'd been running hard, and been able to get a fair amount of water and pick up Gatorade from my husband along the route. Even so, I felt my body beginning to fade. I said to myself: *you're hot and you're not going to make it to the finish line running at this pace in the sun. I have got to slow down.* A mini battle started within me. *If I slow down, I will not run the marathon as fast as I thought I could; but if I slow, I'm fairly sure I can make the finish line. Remember your goal.*

The goal from the very beginning was the finish line in Boston. And so I intentionally slowed down. Keep the goal at the forefront. It can be so tempting to let the glory of the moment distract you from the final objective. Seize the moment, to be sure, but pay attention to what you might be sacrificing. I have always tried to live in the moment, realizing that once that moment was gone, it was gone forever. But the reality of that moment was not what this race was all about. This was a race of strategy for me. I had trained and knew the time I might be able to complete the race in, but I couldn't do that if I ran out of steam. I was there to run the distance and cross the finish line. It was time to slow down so I could do that. My legs relaxed a bit, and my breathing eased. I focused on the next turn in the road and Heartbreak Hill, not too far ahead.

As I slowed my pace, I turned again to the crowd to cheer me on. Those people were wonderful. A couple of times I even heard someone yell out my number coupled with words of encouragement, "You can do it, you can do it."

I kept repeating to myself: *yes, I can do this, I can do this.* Suddenly, I glanced to my right, and there in the crowd was a friend. What an inspiring moment! I had had absolutely no idea he was going to be at the race that day. And, among the thousands of people lining the road to Boston, I picked him out. His eyes caught mine, and we connected. A smile broke forth on his face and he flashed it right in my direction. I caught it, and it was as if he had given me a shot in the arms and legs. I felt an adrenaline rush. How wonderful that, in a mass of humanity, such a simple thing as this could renew my energy.

Of the many things that happened that day, his smile stays with me. Those eyes connecting with mine, almost out of nowhere. I have reflected on that incident. Wondered what the message is for me, for us. What continues to gnaw at me is how often we find ourselves living our days with a busyness that preoccupies our minds and almost in a state of rote actions. We see the crowd and not the faces. We see the faces and not the uniqueness of an individual. We run by and miss the connection. What gift has God given me here? The gift of sight, but am I really using it with all its potential? Focus on the face that is cheering you on, focus on the face that has come out of nowhere, totally at random, and allow it to feed your spirit. Don't run by and see only a blur. Pick out the face that God has put in that time and place to motivate you, to cheer you on, to remind you that you are special in His eyes. You are one of many running this race of life, but you are the unique individual God has made you to be. You can't always, or perhaps ever, be at the front of the pack, but you are running in this race called life. Are you paying attention to God's cheerleaders?

With renewed vigor I turned the corner into the hills of Newton. Heartbreak Hill lay ahead. Up the first hill and then the second. It almost felt good to stretch my legs upward after the course's first half, which had been largely downhill. The Newton Hills would prove to me I was not a fast runner. How could those elite runners bound up the hills in a seemingly effortless manner? I started up infamous Heartbreak Hill, feeling that my lungs would explode and my legs buckle. Where was the top? I struggled to keep pace with the runners around me. Running became extremely hard. Ultimately, I figured I held my own because I stayed with some, passed others, and only allowed a few to run by me. When I got to the top it was there. What was there? The wall. The wall that runners talk about hitting at the twentieth-mile mark because it knocks the energy right out of you. I ran right into it. The runner's wall. Without proper training, a runner can hit this wall, and the race is over for them because of sheer fatigue. I was able to get over—or through the wall depending upon how you look at it—because I had trained to conquer the wall. I was spent beyond my natural limits, but I managed to change gears and begin the run downhill. I could breathe again. My lungs filled. I told myself that I could make it to the finish line. But there was another 10K to go.

Those last miles are a blur to me. Put one foot in front of the other a few more times, and the finish line would be there. I could hardly pick out a single face of the people lining the sidewalks three or four deep down that last stretch of road.

They screamed, "You're almost there, keep it going."

I believed them. I was almost there and knew I had enough strength to keep going to the finish line. My legs ached, my face was white with the salty perspiration that had dried on it, and my whole body was exhausted. The last mile seemed endless.

The sun was low in the sky when I crossed the finish line. I ran across the painted line in the street, stopped my running watch, and hobbled on to the waiting volunteers who covered me with a Mylar blanket. I staggered farther on down the street to a volunteer who hung the "finisher's medal" around my neck.

It was over. The race completed from start to finish. Although my body was numb, I never had felt so alive. I celebrated the fact that my body had held up through 26.2 miles, and all that training had paid off. The elation from deep within gave me a high. I floated off on exhausted legs to find my family.

Life is a challenge. No one would dispute that, because we have all dealt head-on with this truth. What are those challenges? I can name them; you can name them. I have had the privilege of putting the Boston Marathon in that challenge column for myself. It symbolizes for me the ultimate in physical challenges, and in that, it gives me cause to give thanks for the blessing of the human body and all the miracles of its inner workings. Many a challenge in life stems from our physical bodies, for our bodies bear the brunt of this life we live. But in our bodies we know the life with which we have been blessed and gifted by God. Is this precious gift taken for granted? I am not talking just about gaining too much weight, or losing too much weight, or illness and afflictions. I am reflecting on the very life that has been breathed into our physical selves. I am reflecting on the ultimate strength in the body and legs, my lungs that give me air to breathe every step of the way, and my heart that pumps blood, fueling every organ and cell within my body.

Body and Mind

I believe that God presents each of us times when we're called to appreciate our bodies. Something occurs that causes us to pay attention to this tangible gift from God—not only its capabilities but also its limitations. At such times we thank God for the gift of our physical being, yet realize that we're more than that being. At the finish of the Boston Marathon, the time was right to stop and honor the human body, and give thanks for this blessing.

SIXTEEN

The Seminary

"Be still and know that I am God."
Psalm 46:10

God calls. How do we answer? Many of us believe we haven't ever heard a divine call, but perhaps we have and have just not recognized it for what it was. When my children were in elementary school, a glimmer of such an experience began to grow within me. When a friend called and asked me to teach Sunday school, I don't remember why I said yes. I believe now it was more than just fulfilling an obligation to my church and children. My oldest daughter was in the fourth grade, and I thought I could handle that age group. After all, how difficult could the children's questions be?

Within a couple of weeks I realized that I really enjoying talking with kids about the Bible, Jesus, and God. I then started to teach first-graders. I found this teaching even more stirring. The first-graders asked innocently provocative questions that made me stop and think. "If God created the world, who created God?" I found myself often answering them by turning the question back at them: "What do you think?" It was then that a meaningful dialogue would unfold between adult and child. Their answers were often thoughtful and showed their simple understanding of God and who God was to them in their world. Most everything they said made me think harder about my own faith journey.

While growing up I'd attended Sunday school and had gone to worship regularly. I considered myself a "churched" person. I had liked church because my pastor was filled with passion for the gospel, and that passion had been contagious. His sermons drew me in and touched my mind and heart, finding a home in my very being. As I spent a number of years teaching Sunday school, I felt that passion rekindled. I spent a long time preparing for each Sunday school class I taught. This was feeding me, feeding me in a way that only caused me to want more. I must have been hungrier than I imagined.

What teaching Sunday school did ultimately was to propel me toward considering very carefully how God was calling me. If God was calling, how would I answer? How should I respond? I decided to move forward with baby steps.

I had taught Sunday school for about seven years when I decided to take another life-changing step. The idea of seminary intrigued me. *Could I go back to school after so many years away from academia? Would I remember how to write a paper? Would I have the time and discipline to do all the reading that would be demanded of me? What would my family think? Our mother in seminary?* The answer to all those questions lay in taking two classes at seminary: a Christian education class and one in the Old Testament. Those were classes I thought I could handle.

Matriculating to seminary was another hurdle. Looking at the questions the school posed in the admission process intimidated me. Many questions asked about God's call to me. *Had* I been called? I wasn't sure. But when I started to answer the questions, the answers came more easily than I'd expected. When I really thought about where I was and where I potentially might want to go, I realized the journey was not as undefined as I thought. As I reflect back on that time, I can now see God's hand guiding me. I believe that I did not do this on my own. The feeling of God at my side felt more and more real to me.

As I began my new education, I was excited by the courses of study. Balancing my schedule between family, home, and school proved difficult, but something propelled me forward. I absorbed the Old Testament class like a paper towel on a wet surface. When the first paper came due and I received really favorable comments and a good grade on the work, I beamed from ear to ear. Yes. Here was subject matter I could understand. After years of schooling as a youngster, in which I found myself more often than not struggling to grasp various concepts, this course of study I understood. Despite all the distractions, I cranked away at my studies.

As if it were yesterday, I remember that week before Christmas. It marked the end of the first fall semester and also the occurrence of a huge snowstorm in the Boston area. It knocked the power out in our house and all over town. As the hours dragged on, it grew colder and colder. My family sat by a fire to keep warm. I had a final, long paper due that week. Without use of my computer, I scribbled away with pen and paper with fingers like small frigid icicles. Laptop computers were nonexistent, so in a last ditch effort I dragged my entire massive desktop computer to my husband's office, which had power. There I sat trying to block out everything around me as I typed my hand-scribbled research into the computer. The paper got done, but I don't know how. This whole experience felt like a true gift when I handed my work in. And then God gave me a second gift. I aced the paper. With that affirmation, the light turned from amber to green, and I planned for my next semester of classes.

God calls. How do we answer? I answered by registering for more classes and thinking more seriously about graduating from seminary and maybe, just maybe, becoming a pastor.

My seminary education brought forth many challenges of seeking for and searching after answers. Were they from God? That was for me to discern. All these experiences and the discernment process caused me to grow. I have found this to be true in general when we choose to really live life.

The degree program entailed working over the summer as a student chaplain in a hospital. Here the "rubber met the road." In the classroom we talked about and learned theory regarding how to deal with people in differing situations—from the psychology of it to the experiential part. In the hospital there were real people, with very real bodies and with genuine problems of the heart and spirit.

As I look back on that part of my seminary education, I had the faith that God was most assuredly present with me in those days. With many of my chaplain visits, I came to realize that there was a three-way connection going on. I was in the room with the patient, but so, too, was God.

How we all yearn for connection. I have come to understand that whether we are lying in a hospital bed or are as healthy as an ox, we long to connect with people. We can only live on the simple dribble of words for so long before we want to talk about something meaty. We want to share what matters to us, and we want to hear what matters to others. We are searching for a connection that will feed our minds and souls.

This seemed to come easier as folks lay in a hospital bed and a caring pastor was there to listen. But God calls each one of us to have ears to listen. And as we truly hear, God is connecting with us. This is what so many of us in today's world are seeking: making that connection with God that affirms us for who we are and who we can be. That connection with God, which can give meaning and purpose to our lives, has the ability to fill our hearts as we are touched by God's loving hand.

God calls. How do we answer? During my time in seminary, as I sought to find my calling, presence in a community of worship became powerful for me. Prayer, too, became more a part of my everyday life. I was learning the art of prayer in an array of situations. Prayer spilled out of the church and into the lives of the people I was with at that time. But it was at a worship service during those years in seminary that I experienced firsthand the true power of prayer. Describing this incident is almost impossible.

It happened during the pastor's prayer one Sunday morning. The pew felt hard despite the cushion. The room was cold despite my coat. A sense of being by myself overtook me despite the crowded sanctuary. The pastor offered the prayer in a reverent tone. He was allowing and encouraging us to enter into prayer with him. What he was praying for I don't recall. What I do remember is the feeling that came over me as we moved into the time of silent prayer. A tingling sensation and warmth radiated throughout my whole body. This produced a calm within my inner being that I had never felt before. As this feeling enveloped me, I was surprised by the newness of this experience. What is this? And just after I asked this question, I felt and believed this experience was from God. The presence of God moved within me like the warmth of a hot drink finding its way to my stomach and then to my extremities. The comfort felt unbelievably good.

Good feels like such an inadequate word to describe this sensation. But what is *good,* but *God* with another *o* added? Oh, this feeling is powerful, comforting, overwhelming. The connection to the Holy was so strong that day. When I think back on the experience, it blows me away. It felt so profound, I wondered whether it really happened. So how did I answer that presence, that call? By being still and open, believing and trusting. My reaction was not an intellectual exercise but one that came naturally to my whole being. My heart knew just how to guide my body. How I wish I could allow that guidance from the heart more often. Now, when people quote from the psalm, "Be still and know that I am God" (Psalm 46:10), I affirm within myself that I have been there and done that. I have experienced that call and felt the warmth and love. That day in worship I felt at one with God.

As we connect with God, God beckons us to connect to others. As I continued my seminary studies, I increasingly appreciated my family's support. But my new role had to be figured out by all of us. To my husband and children, I had always been a homemaker. I provided meals, washed clothes, chauffeured, and performed the many stay-at-home mother's tasks. Now, suddenly, I was a student. My first semester at seminary, I studied when my children did. I thought that I was acting as a good role model. However, I soon discovered that my family needed, instead, to continue seeing me as Mom. They needed to see me cook, wash clothes, and care for the house. The problem was solved when I reversed my schedule. As soon as my children left the house for school each day, I sat down to study. When they walked through the door in the afternoon, I did motherly tasks. In their eyes my role was restored. So was the stability of family life. My family would grow into my role as pastor. Over the next four years, we'd grow together. Was all this figuring out a product of my doing? Probably not. I believe God was calling, and He was going to help me figure out how to best answer that call at that time in my life.

If God was calling me to the pastorate, then I was going to have to learn how to be comfortable in my new role. With this discernment I went forth into a church other than my own to do field education ministry. Leaving my church friends who had wholeheartedly supported me was unsettling. I had worked now for many years in a familiar surrounding in which there was great comfort. To be thrown into another world with different ideas and beliefs, practices and history was to help me grow in my call. God was calling: find another church—and so I did. The people of my new church didn't know me as a mother of four, wife of a newspaper publisher, runner, and lover of gardening. They knew me as their student pastor. The amount of trust they put to me when I arrived on their doorstep almost scared me.

Was God calling me to a certain authority? Most certainly the people at my new church gave me an authority I had not known before. I was their pastor, a student pastor, but nonetheless a pastor with all the "rights and privileges." I struggled with that new role. How was I to use this authority? When was I to use it? Did I really know that much more than the people I had been called to serve? Would I grow into this new authority? Jesus had the true authority that was rightly from God: "They were astounded at his teaching, because he spoke with authority . . . They were all amazed and kept saying to one another, 'What kind of utterance is this? For with authority and power he commands the unclean spirits, and out they come!' " (Luke 4:32, 36). How could I come to understand better this new authority given to me through God's call? My experiences of pastoring a church would be my guideposts.

As I struggled with this new authority, so too did I struggle with authenticity. Authenticity is learning all about the self. It is about not fearing the real self but acknowledging the self as human and therefore acknowledging the shortcomings of a created being. There was no question that I wanted to do the best I could in my church work and ministry. But to be truly authentic I needed to accept that I was vulnerable and had weaknesses, even as God was calling me. In my year of field education in this church and in my years of study in seminary, I came to better understand the power in weakness. St. Paul recorded the Lord's words to him as he wrote to the church in Corinth, "My grace is sufficient for you, for my power is made perfect in weakness" (2 Corinthians 12:9). I would find a truer relationship with the people to whom I was pastoring. Vulnerability and weakness were the bridge to better understanding and relationships with people. Through this understanding, my relationship with God through Christ truly grew. As I allowed any mask I had worn to come off and the people could see and feel the real me (which is truly less than perfect), I felt a growing faith in Christ's presence with me and within the congregation I was serving.

A large part of my field education was the process of discerning my call with the church I was then working in. And so with my new church I began to delve into the question of God's call and how I experienced that. The committee that worked with me in my new role was eager to find out about me. We had long conversations about the running of their church but also the process of discerning God's call. They asked again and again, "How do you know it's from God? Can you really hear God calling to you, speaking to you?" Those were thought-provoking questions, for all of us. So often this journey felt like a whole new land I was exploring. Turning over every rock and stone to find the way became a job in itself. Was I looking under the right rocks and stones to find God's call? Or should I just charge ahead and try my hand at everything in my path? Discernment, discernment. I reflect on the many roles we're called to assume. Does God call us to particular roles? I believed that God had called me to this new church, but I wondered what part God played in our ability to discern our proper roles in life. God calls. How do we answer?

The question arises, *are we locked into roles in our lives?* Do we lock ourselves into those roles? If so, how do we do that or allow it to happen? And if we do, do we want to change, and so how do we begin initiating these changes? I reflect on the properties of water. Depending upon the season, water takes on a different form. In the winter it creates a blanket of white on which to ski or a glimmering pond covered in ice for us to skate upon. Come spring, it falls from the sky and brings forth rebirth from the previously frozen ground. In the summer, water forms a steam rising off a hot path. In the autumn, a mist gathers as the earth begins again to cool off.

There are seasons in our lives. Perhaps that's part of what makes life so full and interesting. In each of these seasons we are called to take on a role, but as the years unfold God calls us to renew—perhaps to take on different roles. We are the ones who allow ourselves to get stuck. We push the inner urgings of our God out of our hearts. We are the ones who must be open, willing to change, and ready to listen, because God is a living and active God and so calls us anew each new day and in each new season.

Seminary helped me to discern my call. But the experience continues to beg certain questions from me. What is a divine call? Is it really from God? How do we know that for sure? And what does it feel like? I believe this demands a better understanding of the self. Who are you? If you listen to all the people around you and all the experiences you have had, this discovery begins to take shape. The key is opening up, listening, and being ready to be transformed by God. With open ears and eyes, minds and hearts, we can discern our call—with God's help.

SEVENTEEN

The Chaplaincy

"Nothing will be impossible with God."
Luke 1:17

I put away the books from my Master of Divinity program for a summer of hands-on experiences. To graduate I needed to earn credits in Clinical Pastoral Education (CPE). The course could be spread over a year or completed in one eight-week summer program. Choosing the latter, I started applying to hospital chaplaincy programs in the spring. To my delight I was accepted at my first choice, St. Elizabeth's Hospital, one of the premier CPE sites in my area.

My hospital schedule would be 9 a.m. to 5 p.m. on weekdays plus a couple of weekends and night shifts. The program was known to be intense, therefore I got my home life in order so that I could concentrate purely on my hospital chaplaincy.

With excitement, but some trepidation, I headed out to the hospital that first morning. I wanted to get off to a good start and so gave myself what I thought would be enough time to get there. Turns out, I went the long way and got stuck in the morning traffic. I sat pounding the steering wheel, cursing my stupidity, fearful that I would be late. I got to the hospital on time but already frazzled. All I could think was *this is going to be a very long summer*.

As I walked the halls, looking for the meeting room, I tried to calm down and focus. To my relief, I wasn't the last to arrive. Others, too, had been delayed.

Body and Mind

Little did we all know that that would be the first of many experiences in finding our way into new situations and places this summer. Hospital ministry loomed before us. The transforming work of chaplaincy stood at the door and welcomed us into its world.

We were a diverse group of men and women, numbering ten with two advisors and one supervisor. Each morning began with a short worship service conducted by one of us. That first morning I was singing praises to the Lord that I had made it in one piece and giving thanks for my colleagues and advisors, of whom I would grow very fond. We all came from different backgrounds and had different histories and agendas, but we shared a passion for God's message and work. Chaplaincy would prove to be contagious and life giving.

As I reflect back on that summer, I recall some of my many experiences. How to express them? As I write this, there is no particular order or priority for these recollections. I write as they come to mind. I reflect as they touch my heart one more time. I hear God's call to His people to care for one another, and so I revisit once more what I learned that summer: what I learned about human beings. What I learned about people in hospitals. What I learned about people offering care. What I learned about myself. What I learned about my very inner being, heart and soul. What I learned about this journey of faith I was on. Every experience in its own way opened a new door and invited me to learn, to experience, to grow, to be transformed. The mysteries of the art of healing and wholeness stood before me. With an open heart I ran to greet and learn from them.

That first week there were many meaningful discussions in our classroom. As a group, we went on guided tours of the hospital to acquaint us with the layout of where we'd be working for the rest of the summer. Being in a group provided a certain comfort. We didn't have any responsibilities yet. As we walked through the halls, we wore our passion for ministry under our blouses and shirts, burning within us, but concealed to the rest of the world. There would be time enough to show our caring and learn how to care.

At the end of week one we were given our first assignment to visit with the patients. "This may not be that easy for some of you," our advisors told us frankly. "The first step is to make it to the elevator. The next step is to get on that elevator and ride it to the right floor. The next step is to get off the elevator, and find your way to the patient's room. If you can go in, that's great, but if you can't, that's okay, too. There will be another day. When you're ready, you will know it. If this whole process scares you, your trust and faith in God's presence and guidance will get you into the patient's room." How difficult could this be? I had been in lots of hospitals and spent a month in one as a patient, so I didn't anticipate any difficulty. However, my eyes opened fast.

I found the elevator that led to the floor to which I had been assigned, pushed the button, and waited for the doors to open. When they opened, I got on and pushed the button for the floor I wanted. I rode up in silence, and my nerve began to wane. The doors opened, and I didn't get out. I rode the elevator to the next stop and got off pretending everything was fine and this was my destination. I took a deep breath and said a prayer. Then I took the elevator back to the correct floor. This time I got off and walked down the hall toward the rooms of my assigned patients. I glanced into rooms that I passed. I got to the nurses station and introduced myself. The nurses were pleasant and very welcoming. They had been this route before with other seminary students. I could feel their reaching out to me with reassurance. Their smiles were a welcome step. Still, I couldn't bring myself to visit any patients that day, but I did make it to the floors. As I drove home that night I assured myself that next time it would be easier.

So, what's so difficult about visiting a person in a hospital room? I could rationalize a couple of things. First of all, I wouldn't know this person from Adam. Second, I was worried they couldn't care less about me. Third, they might even resent the fact that I had come at all. Fourth, they might be in such a compromised condition that I would physically be taken aback and start to feel badly myself. Fifth, I wasn't sure what to say or how to begin. Sixth, how would they react to an unannounced Protestant pastor? The list went on and on in my mind. Mostly, I feared that I wouldn't be able to help. Herein would ultimately be the real learning experience for me. Tomorrow I would visit my first patient.

With building confidence, the next day I got off the elevator and headed for the nurses station and told them that I'd be visiting patients. As I stood at the entrance to the first room, I had a momentary flashback. It gave me pause: there was a woman lying in the bed, and that woman was me. She was covered with pure white sheets and a white blanket. She lay perfectly still, seemingly gazing into space. Lost in the moment. I could see my face in her face. A sort of

"I can't believe this is happening to me" look was apparent. I felt the pain, loneliness, and fear I had endured during my month-long hospitalization ten years before. The past came racing back and grabbed me right in the heart. Why didn't I go into any of the rooms yesterday? Standing there, I now understood why. It was not about the fears I had conjured up in my mind yesterday, but about the pain of the past. Would I relive my own hospitalization with every room I entered? I was not sure but prayed that God would give me the strength and courage to do this hospital ministry.

After that first room, I worked my way down the hall stopping in to visit with each patient. All the patients welcomed me. I encouraged them to tell me about themselves, knowing most people are eager to talk about themselves. Conversations came easily and most patients were delighted by the visit. My confidence was building.

As the visits unfolded over the weeks, I encountered fascinating stories. Some were tied into faith journeys, others into courage, others into loneliness or anxiety, and still others into fear and dread. One afternoon an elderly man invited me to pull up a chair. He had a story to tell. "I was brought back to life," he began.

"That is so wonderful," I said innocently.

"It was truly amazing." He then proceeded to tell me about his near-death experience. He had been brought into the emergency room suffering from a heart attack. He remembered the technicians and doctors working on him. He remembered the room going black. And then he said he saw a light. He was walking toward the light. In the light he felt a warmth, comfort, and peace as he moved toward the light. "It just felt really good," he told me. "And then I woke up."

He later learned that in those moments the doctors had believed they had lost him and he had died. "Through the miracles of medicine and by the grace of God, I was brought back to life." He believed he had died and then walked toward God, the light.

I sat spellbound as he told me his story. *Could this really be? Does this really happen?* He was so sure it had happened and he had seen God. I read in the Old Testament book of Genesis, "Is anything too wonderful for the Lord?" (Genesis 18:14). As if in answer, Luke wrote, "Nothing will be impossible with God" (Luke 1:17). I have heard of such incidences happening as this man described and read about them in books, but here I was sitting next to a person who had actually had such an experience. Through faith I trusted in his words. Through faith I have embraced the mystery in this story. Through faith I have come to believe that nothing is impossible with God. If ever there was a faith lesson for me, this was one of them.

For one week I was on the oncology floor. The horrors of cancer hit home big-time. Bald and mumbling incoherently, affected by her drug treatment, a woman sat in bed. She had no idea who I was or why I was there. Finally, I stopped talking and asking questions. As I got up to leave, I asked one last question: "Do you want to pray?" She looked me in the eyes and nodded. As I looked into her eyes and saw that she felt lost, my heart ached. I silently prayed to myself, "Dear God, give me the strength and wisdom to bring you to her. Let me be your messenger of hope and love." I reached toward the woman, and she took my hands.

Her grasp was shaky but firm. I took a deep breath and allowed the words of the prayer to come. I thought I knew what to say, but mysteriously the words took on a life of their own and tumbled out of my mouth in a rhythmic fashion, without planning or effort on my part. A calmness settled over me, and I felt a strong hold from her, but it was of peace, not fighting. When I let go, we gazed for a moment into each other's eyes. Her face said, "thank you." As I left I assured her I would be back tomorrow, and I knew I would. I reflect back now that as I walked down the hall away from her room, I began to believe more and more that indeed with God everything is possible.

One evening I entered a room in which a middle-aged woman lay in bed in a fetal position. I approached the bed to see if she was asleep. She must have sensed movement in the room, because she looked up at me and immediately began to cry. As the scene started to unfold, a part of me wanted to turn away and leave, because I sensed this would be too difficult. The other part said pull up a chair next to her, because here was a person I could really help in her moment of despair. She called me over. She needed desperately to talk to someone, anyone. I explained who I was and the floodgates opened. She poured her heart out to me. All I did was sit there and try to take it all in.

As she went on and on, all I wanted to do was fix it. How could I fix her? How could I fix the situation she was in? Where were the answers? There must be a way. Interestingly enough, as I told my colleagues about this situation the following day at our debriefing meeting, I mentioned that mine was a desire to fix, not necessarily heal. Why fix? Because I had a lot of experience and training in fixing things. How is that? I was a mother of four, and isn't a mother constantly called upon to fix things? Mothers fix things that are broken in the house. Mothers fix things associated with school and community. Mothers fix the broken hearts of their children. Aren't mothers expected to make it all right? To make it better? I know I have always tried, and for the most part believed I was pretty good at fixing things.

I also had experience as an Emergency Medical Technician (EMT). I'd served on the town ambulance for more than six years by this time. Every time I was called to an accident scene, I was expected to fix the injured. I bandaged, diagnosed, and consoled. I fixed the person long enough to get them to the hospital. To watch a life slip away from you, when you have been trained to save, is really difficult. I was expected to be good at my job, because "fixing" might mean life over death. Fixing things came spontaneously to me. Yet I couldn't fix this woman. With all my expertise, there was within me a sense of helplessness.

That summer at the hospital, this strong desire to fix everything was one of the biggest hurdles for me in learning to be a hospital chaplain and pastor. I had to stop trying, and even wanting, to fix the patients. What I had to learn was how to be a presence for them. How to just be there for them. Not to fix but to *be*. Not healing but wholeness of being. I had no power to heal, but within my grasp was the power to instill wholeness in those I encountered in the hospital. The wholeness I speak of is not from an earthly dimension but from the spiritual one. Wholeness grows through the acceptance of God's grace, through faith in God, through Jesus Christ and living in the knowledge of God's love for humankind and creation. Jesus again and again asks us to bring to him all who are weary and carry a burden. Through a relationship with him we can move to wholeness which trumps fixing and healing because of the power of peace, comfort, and love it carries with it. Such is the promise of our Lord.

God calls us to first *be* and then *act*. God calls us to be Christ's hands and heart in the here and now. Since that memorable summer, slowly I have come to trust the Holy Spirit more and more to lead me in that being. I want to heal.

We all want to heal a broken or suffering person. I now have the faith that it is in my presence that I can heal. Not a medical healing, but a healing of heart and soul that comes through being. It is a healing of wholeness that comes with putting your faith in God through the power and presence of Christ dwelling within you.

An elderly white-haired woman more fully taught me the power of presence. I visited her one afternoon about halfway through my summer at the hospital. She had the most wonderful smile. The kind that invited you into the room and into her heart. Because she was initially so open and chatty it was easy for me to sit with her. We talked for quite a while. I was aware of the length of time I had been with her and started to excuse myself. She then made the request of me that started me down a new path in my journey of faith.

"Just sit with me for a while longer," she said. "We don't have to talk. Matter of fact, I don't want to talk any longer. I just want you with me."

I pulled the chair back up to her bedside and sat down. She didn't look at me, and I didn't look at her. We did not hold hands, as I often did with patients. We just sat together in a quiet sense of being. I remember I was a bit uncomfortable at first, but this presence, one to another, began to grow within me. It felt comfortable and really right. There was a warmth in our connectedness of presence. I learned a lot that afternoon. My faith in just being a vehicle of God's love and comfort through presence grew and has continued to transform my being.

As the summer drew to a close, I realized that my own hospitalization more than a decade earlier had been a help rather than a hindrance. Because of it I could relate, I could empathize. I couldn't be in the patient's shoes, but I could walk in the shoes I had known and so understood better what they were feeling and going through. I knew how hard it was to lie in a hospital bed at the mercy of the doctors and medical world. I had known all this pain. I knew what it had done to me physically and emotionally. I knew how important a visit and a kind touch or word could be. I had known the power of presence and what it was like to live without it. My faith had grown during that time of hospitalization and now was continuing to transform my ministry, and even more my ability to be with others.

Body and Mind

With all the rushing around, visiting of patients, and CPE reports to be written, life that summer seemed overwhelming at times. It was the elderly white-haired lady that brought the words of the psalmist into my heart forever. She taught me one of my greatest lessons that summer and perhaps in all my ministry: "Be still and know that I am God" (Psalm 46:10). I need that in my life, because when I heed those words I know the power of being. I know the power of presence. My presence in another's life and the presence of God through Christ in mine. In the stillness of life and heart we can and will truly know God.

EIGHTEEN

Preaching

"This is the day that the Lord has made."
Psalm 118:24

That Sunday morning dawned bright, with a crisp feel to the air that signaled autumn. As I walked down my driveway I couldn't help but notice the trees. Most had adorned themselves in fall wardrobes of oranges, reds, and browns. As the sunlight hit my face, I thought to myself, "This is the day that the Lord has made. Let us rejoice and be glad in it" (Psalm 118:24). It was refreshing to go for a run, clear my head, and try to relax. This Sunday had been looming on the horizon now for a couple of weeks, carrying with it excitement and nerves. I was to preach my first sermon today. Was I prepared? I certainly hoped so, but only time would tell.

I had entered seminary the previous fall. I thought I'd heard God's voice, but needed to find out if this was truly the direction for me. Up to this Sunday I had taken only four courses, purely of my own choosing and interest. Preaching most certainly had not been one of them. So why was I then preaching this Sunday?

Tom, the senior pastor of my church, was scheduled to take his fall vacation and needed someone to fill the pulpit on the Sunday he would be gone. He had asked me. I felt honored. Tom had encouraged me to take some classes at seminary, so I knew I had his support and respect for my new faith journey. He told me he had every confidence that I would do a fine job. That was so good to hear, but I wondered if he would be right. There was one major obstacle. One really big obstacle. I was scared to death to speak in public. I had always avoided it like the plague. Looking for someone to read in church? Not me. Looking for someone to give the announcements at the meeting? Not me. Someone to stand up in front of a large group of people and talk? Not me. This was not my thing. I could work magic behind the scenes, but speak in public? Not me.

I felt a kindred spirit with Moses and the Old Testament prophet Jeremiah. Moses was called to lead his enslaved people out of Egypt to the Promised Land. This was to be the defining act of the Old Testament, and yet he comes before the Lord God saying, "O my Lord, I have never been eloquent, neither in the past nor even now . . . I am slow of speech and slow of tongue" (Exodus 4:10). Moses' words resonated in my ear.

The Lord God gave Moses his brother Aaron to speak for him. I was under no illusion that there would be an Aaron for me. I was to open my mouth and speak to the people. The prophet Jeremiah, too, pled with the Lord God: "Ah, Lord God! Truly I do not know how to speak, for I am only a boy" (Jeremiah 1:7). I was certainly no boy, but a young woman fearful of speaking in public. I truly wondered if I could speak before my congregation, let alone with any passion. The ironic thing about being asked to stand in front and deliver a sermon was that I really wanted to do it. I wanted to preach the Word of God. From where was I to derive *my* help?

My public speaking career began on an earlier Sunday by just having the nerve to stand up at a worship service and read the opening words from the bulletin. I emphasize *read,* because that's all I had to do. I didn't even have to look at the people. No one would see my knees shaking behind the lectern under the cover of a clerical robe. I only had to walk a mere seven feet from the chair to the lectern, without tripping and wavering. I could do that. Could I do that? It can't be that hard. Surely my nerves could stand those brief minutes as everyone looked up at me and listened to the words spilling out of my mouth. Here was another requirement. The words had to be audible and exact, because the congregation would be reading silently along with me from the service bulletin. How hard could that be? Felt pretty hard in the very beginning.

Misery loves company, the old saying goes. To add to the fear of just reading, I decided I wanted to begin with my own words before launching into the printed material in the service order. The psalmist's words, "This is the day that the Lord has made. Let us rejoice and be glad in it," had always been among my favorite Scriptures. That is where I wanted to start. To begin by giving glory to the Lord for the gift of another day. Before I stepped up to the lectern the very first time, I rehearsed those words over and over. I whispered them. When no one was near, I said them aloud, to assess my voice and tone. I even printed them out in large type so that I'd be able to look down and read them if my memory failed. Not the best option, but it made me feel more comfortable.

My knees shook, and I felt weak that first time in front of the congregation, but I got through it. I looked down at the papers more than I wanted, but my voice didn't crack, and I was still standing when the opening words, which lasted all of about two minutes, were over. It never felt so good to sit down and fade into the background as attention was turned away from me to the pastor. After the service everyone was so kind and said how nice it was to see me up front. I wasn't so sure about the up front part, but it was a beginning and I had to start somewhere.

I need more help with this public speaking, I said to myself after a Sunday or two of being up front: *Where else can I find some help?* My husband suggested a public speaking course. Why not give it a try? And so I went in search for one. I signed up for a class, not far from my home, that would meet once a week for six weeks. I really didn't know what to expect but went with an open mind and eager spirit, confident that I wouldn't get much out of this class unless I put a lot into it.

At the first session, the few people who had enrolled sat in a circle. We introduced ourselves and gave a reason for wanting to take the class. To know I was not alone in my fear of public speaking was comforting. Rationally, I had known that, but it was therapeutic to confess my fear and hear others do likewise. Confident and knowledgeable, the instructor showed skill and ease when speaking in front of people. This is going to be good, I encouraged myself. I might even enjoy these six weeks, as well as gain some poise and confidence standing in front of people. The lessons had begun.

Body and Mind

We went through a lot of theory, much of which I knew through general reading and suggestions people had offered over the years. No sooner had we begun than we were asked to prepare and deliver a low-key presentation on a subject of our choice. It was to be no more than five minutes. We were to jot our main ideas on note cards and speak with no other notes. I prepared as instructed. As I sat there in the small classroom I was still nervous. I wanted to say to myself, "Oh, come on! You'll never see these people again and how much worse can I be than my classmates?" I was right.

The first woman to present did extremely poorly. And I thought I was going to do badly! Patiently, I persevered through her speech. Of note, she would make considerable progress during the course. I nervously awaited my turn. However, once I started to speak, I covered the material fairly well. As the weeks went by, I gathered more and more confidence. At the end of the class, I was pleased with the help I had gotten, but this was only a small classroom. My ultimate destination: the pulpit of a church with, potentially, a full sanctuary. That could mean two hundred people.

At least I knew well in advance when I was to preach my first sermon. I set about preparing; I wrote a first draft and shared it with Tom. I knew he could and would be a big help with the content. If I had confidence in what I was going to say, I rationalized it might make the delivery that much easier. Tom read it, and we dissected it. I noticed how he was respectful of my message and careful not to change it. I reworked the questionable parts, and we went through it again. My confidence was building. My confidence really took hold when I stood by a section of the sermon he felt was not as good as it could be. I argued that this was my sermon, not his. Even if I had all the help in the world available, I didn't want to be a copycat. The words had to come from my heart in my own style. I left the section unchanged, and, in the end, it worked well in the overall message.

It was up to me now, or so I thought. The week before my sermon, I continually reviewed the text. I printed it out in a large font, leaving spaces at critical points along the way. *I can do this,* I kept telling myself. *If all else fails, I can read it.* But I wanted to do more than just that. I wanted to launch my preaching career in a respectable manner. This first sermon felt like a big step for me. Surprisingly, I recall sleeping well that Saturday night. I really thought I would be tossing and turning with anxiety.

And then the bright, crisp Sunday morning. As I put my feet on the floor, I rehearsed my opening line: *This is the day that the Lord has made. Let us rejoice and be glad in it.* I prayed it may be so. When I arrived at the church, I was drawn into all the preworship preparations. Readying the sanctuary distracted me from the nervousness I had been feeling. I placed my manuscript on the pulpit and flipped through it one last time. I looked out at the pews, and there were already a few early arrivers. I smiled at them and they returned the greeting.

The service began as I walked the aisle to find my place up front. As I turned around and sat down, I looked out. It was a smaller crowd because of the holiday weekend, but that was okay. *Baby steps, baby steps into the pulpit,* I told myself. As the organ music concluded, I prayed fervently. I prayed for strength, courage, wisdom. I prayed for anything and everything I thought would get me through the service and in particular my sermon. As I stood before the congregation for the first time that morning, I gave it all up to God.

As I finally started my sermon, I remember feeling far more comfortable than I'd expected. The opening words went well. I moved on and the momentum began to build. I looked intentionally at different people and watched their faces. The congregants responded with their eyes, and the eye contact strengthened rather than intimidated me. That was very heartening. Instead of standing stiffly, as I'd feared I might, I moved naturally in the pulpit. I could use my hands and arms to talk with, as well as my mouth. By the last page of the sermon, I felt energized and tried to convey my closing thoughts with the passion that was burning within me. When the final *amen* was offered, I was relieved that I had made it through my first sermon, but also overwhelmed by a sense of presence.

As I have spent the years reflecting back on this first sermon I preached, I believe without a doubt I could not have done it by myself. Yes, I had had the help of teachers and friends, but ultimately help had come through the presence of God. What I had been feeling was the power from an ever-present God. There was a presence with me that morning that is difficult to put into words. That presence cast a shadow of warmth over me, not of darkness, but an aura of light. It was something I had never experienced before. It filled me with passion for the love of God. God's love was incredibly powerful and present that morning for me. As I continue my faith journey, I have come to believe in that love of God more and more through my growing relationship with Jesus Christ.

Body and Mind

Jesus said, "I am the vine, you are the branches. Those who abide in me and I in them bear much fruit, because apart from me you can do nothing" (John 15:5). These words took on new meaning that Sunday morning and have continued to transform me and my spiritual journey. I realized that there are, in fact, some things you just cannot do by yourself. Family, friends, the world lend a helping hand, but there are times when we need to reach beyond that to a help far more powerful and present and loving. To abide in Christ is to transform your inner being. It is to grow your heart into a whole new dimension with a whole new dynamic. As I have allowed that presence, which I felt that Sunday morning, to guide and fill me, I have come to better understand and feel my trust and faith.

After the service people complimented me for a job well done. But how does one truly measure accomplishment? Is there a sliding scale from one to ten? Is it judged by the reactions? Is it in the physical pleasure or worldly goods obtained? Is it in the pat on the back you give yourself for that something you controlled and did well? Maybe accomplishment appears in many different faces. Many of these faces make us feel good, and perhaps they are well deserved. But for me, if I put all my money in these baskets, I still feel a sense of emptiness. I have felt the shadow of warmth over me, the aura of light that I believe comes only from God. It is in this shadow where I feel the true gift of life. As I have allowed this to fill me, I have found a greater and greater desire to pass along that light. For, as we know, when light is divided and shared, it does not diminish, but rather it grows. Through a growing faith and trust in God through Christ, the true measure of accomplishment for me has come from the passing along of the light of God, a light that gives meaning, comfort and peace to life. The message of God's love for us all.

I accomplished something that Sunday morning, but not on my own and not of this world. The presence of God's help and love took up residence in my heart and, even now, continues to build a dwelling there with a stronger and stronger foundation transforming my spiritual journey and how I try to live my life. It is with thanksgiving and praise for God's help that I recall that crisp Sunday morning when nature was redressing herself in her splendid autumn wardrobe and I preached my very first sermon.

NINETEEN

The Books

"The one who hears the word"
Matthew 13:23

Like many days this summer, the day dawned with bright sunshine. The air was warm with a slight breeze. The beach was very inviting, but I had a desire to go to worship this Sunday morning.

As I entered the sanctuary, I found it already more than half full. A young family came in and sat in the pew in front of me. In the pew to my left, two elderly women found their place. People walked to the front to find a seat. By ten o'clock the church was almost full. Watching the people coming in, I thought, *A good turnout for a beautiful summer morning.* As a visitor in this church, I was impressed by the number of people and children who had come to worship. I wanted to believe we had all come from our summer's activities to give thanks and praise to God for the many gifts we had received.

The service began with upbeat singing and moved quickly along to the sermon. The pastor came down from the altar to preach among us. The Scripture lesson was the parable of the sower from the gospel of Matthew. It was a good story to talk about on such a day, if for no other reason than Jesus' parable was delivered from a boat to people standing on a beach. As the pastor went along, I felt drawn into his message. Jesus said:

> Listen! A sower went out to sow. And as he sowed, some seeds fell on the path, and the birds came and ate them up. Other seeds fell on rocky ground, where they did not have much soil, and they sprang up quickly, since they had no depth of soil. But when the sun rose, they were scorched; and since they had no root, they withered away. Other seeds fell among thorns, and the thorns grew up and choked them. Other seeds fell on good soil and brought forth grain, some a hundredfold, some sixty, some thirty. Let anyone with ears listen! (Matthew 13:3–9)

This is good, I thought, *here are the seeds, sun, and growth of summer.* The sermon touched me.

In this parable Jesus speaks about the word of God and how people hear and receive it. The final verse of the Scripture lesson, which offers an interpretation of the parable, resonated with me and caused me to reflect back to an incident that occurred during the winter of the year. "But as for what was sown on good soil, this is the one who hears the word and understands it, who indeed bears fruit and yields, in one case a hundredfold, in another sixty, and in another thirty" (Matthew 13:23). That is, God's word has great power for those who take it unto themselves and go forth and live it. I reflected. Word: the power of the word of God found in the books of the Bible. Words: the power of words found in books of the past and present. As I left worship that morning, I found myself drifting back six months, thinking about books and words.

It was an unbelievably charming place. As my sister and I entered her favorite bookstore, I was taken in by the charm of the space and the hundreds of books displayed in such a creative fashion. It was a huge room with all-natural wood walls, ceiling, and bookcases. It looked like a funky old barn, but was actually a theater that had been renovated into this awesome bookstore. I walked among the shelves of books, whose colorful dust jackets stood out boldly against the wood. Blues offset reds; gold print highlighted greens. The large room emanated an invitation to come see, come explore what lies within these walls and on these shelves. At first I just roamed around. My sister went in one direction and I in another. I went down a few steps into a sunken area that had been the theater's orchestra pit and then out the other side toward the former stage, to further investigate the huge variety of books.

As I moved among the shelves, I found myself walking into different worlds. What were in all those books? Here were books of history, to the right were books of romance, and over there were books of real people and, to the left, books of fantasy. In some I knew I would find tears and in others laughter. I would find emotion and learning, witness and facts. At the end of one aisle there was a woman absorbed in a book. *Weren't you supposed to buy the book before you read it?* I thought. But the atmosphere in the place invited you to explore and read at your leisure. I found myself lost in the world of titles and stories. I found myself lost in the greatness of books and all therein.

Within this bookstore there were hundreds and hundreds of stories. *In the narrative are the secrets of life,* I thought, *to tell a story is to give meaning.* As I took in the book titles, I thought about the many books I've read, from biography to science fiction. And what about the escape of a romance or fantasy? I have always loved escapist literature.

As I reflected on the books, I realized that in each word there was the possibility of enrichment of mind and heart, soul and life. I felt the humanness of it. Here is humanity stretched out in facts and emotions, questions and answers. Here are worlds to explore. Here is a chance to escape. There is a chance to learn. There is a chance to grow. Even within the large children's section there were those opportunities and possibilities. As I checked out this section, I was intrigued by the creativity of those reading materials. As I held a toddler's hardcover book, I thought of the worlds that children would discover as it was being read to them. The pictures spoke a million words. The child's imagination would begin to blossom and grow.

I found my sister studying the books in the novel section. When she noticed me standing next to her, she began telling me about the books. She told me a bit about one author and then another. We then walked together around the other side of the store and, as we walked, she pointed out the different authors she knew of. I was impressed by her wealth of knowledge about the authors and their books. As we moved along, her love of books and words emerged so very clearly. I was overwhelmed by the knowledge of writing at her fingertips. This was her world. This was her passion. This was her expertise. Here before us was the power of books and of the word.

It was so truly wonderful to step into my sister's world. So much of my world has been a physical one with all the athletics I have been involved in. I have done my share of reading and studying but not even close to the amount of reading my sister has done. It was magical to step into her world. I felt like an invited guest being given a private tour.

I believe each one of us lives so much in our own worlds that, at times, we forget about the other worlds. To step into another's world, into another's life, can be eye-opening. In taking this step I have always found that my mind and spirit find growth through that of others. I have discovered little pieces of myself that lay hidden or unused. I find a connection.

In a world that moves so fast and can be so impersonal, I have come to believe that people seek connections. Connections are made every day, but most never get below the surface. We connect via phone, BlackBerry, or computer, but it's the deep connections that have the meaning for life. It's when we are invited into the very being and inner self of another that we connect. Relationships through work, sports, or service are valuable, but it is the deeper relationships that bring companionship and healing, joy and love. The relationship that carries the adjective "sacred" is the most life-sustaining, life-giving one. This comes about when a world is shared in common. This day in this place I viewed my relationship with my sister as sacred. Sacred not as holy, but as set apart. Set apart, as the relationship is special and the connection as blessed.

As I reflect further, I pause to ponder the sacredness of words. Returning to the parable of the sower, it is the word of God falling upon good soil that truly bears fruit and yields a hundredfold. God's word is sacred. In faith I have endeavored to cultivate good soil and sow the seeds of God's sacred word and, from there, grow a sacred relationship with God through Christ. Here the sacred is the Holy. As the sacred words of Scripture flow from my Bible, I try to listen—to really listen with open eyes, ears, and heart. What is this story I am hearing? What is the message? Where is the connection?

And if I am bold enough, what is the meaning for me and the world? Who is the author? This last question is perhaps the easiest to answer. Who is the author? In this book, the Bible, it is God. Therein lies the power of words, the power of the Word.

As my mind's eye flashes back to all those books in my sister's favorite bookstore, I am warmed and brought to a certain joy at the connection I feel. A connection to the world of words, a connection to my sister and, with an ever-seeking heart, my connection with Christ through God's Word.

Heart and Soul

TWENTY

Love

"Enter his gates with thanksgiving"
Psalm 100:4

There is a great mystery in love. We gathered in the kitchen midmorning Thanksgiving Day last year. I often wonder why we gravitate toward the kitchen. Many other rooms in my house have comfortable chairs and couches, places conducive to conversation. Maybe it's the warmth of the kitchen that draws us there. Maybe it's because this is where I inevitably find myself. Maybe it's because we love to eat and sharing a meal is often what brings us together. I smile when I see us gathered in the kitchen that Thanksgiving. Amid the chatter, smoke pours out of the stove, creating a large white cloud, engulfing all of us.

Why are we drawn to stay in the kitchen? Is it a fear of the house going up in smoke? I wonder. What would we do if the flames broke forth from the oven? Would we have the wherewithal to reach for the phone and dial 911? And then when the voice came on the line, have the cool to be clear about what was happening and where the fire was? I realize the police can now trace calls. They would find us. I'm just wondering aloud.

If the flames did engulf the kitchen, I thought about what I would do first. Would I question whether this was a nightmare or the house was truly going up in flames? My children stood with me and chatted, oblivious to this smoke, as if its presence was not usual. Not to worry, they trusted me. Would love keep us safe? What a crazy thought. Did they believe that I loved them enough to never let anything happen to them? Would I? Or was it easier to make light of the smoke-filled kitchen rather than push the panic button. A curious thing.

Maybe they were staying in the kitchen, because they wanted to show their support for Mom. How deep does support run in the streams of love? They seemed to be willing to stand there in the smoke and carry on conversations as if nothing were happening. The smoke continued to pour out of the stove, and they continued to support my feeble attempts to rid the room of the cloud. How strange it felt. Open the windows, open the doors, turn on the fan. That they would persevere, laugh with me, and support me in my misjudgment of the situation touched my heart.

Or did we love each other's company so much that we would die bravely together in this familiar kitchen? I was not entirely sure why they chose to continue to hang out with me, but I had a strange sense of calm. No, the situation was not ideal but, in their company, I could cope.

Maybe the wondrous mystery of love is that we have within us the capability of standing with another even when things go wrong, and most particularly when it seems as if all is lost. There is a powerful presence in another's company when the room is filling with smoke. In our laughter—yes, there was laughter—over the whole predicament, a closeness pervaded. We were together, dealing with a situation less than ideal. The mystery of love noted in such a weird situation brought a strange sense of calm for me. At long last, my daughter, Elizabeth, suggested we turn the oven off and put it on a clean cycle.

Brilliant. Crisis averted.

But only to face the next challenge just around the corner.

As we ate lunch together, the cleaning cycle of the oven continued to whirr. The kitchen emptied out, and so I found myself doing dishes, packing away the leftovers, and thinking about what next to prepare for dinner. Where had that mystery of love found in the cloud of smoke gone? Elizabeth appeared to help cut up the stuffing, but was quickly drawn back into the conversation and play in the next room. The kitchen felt big and empty; I felt lonely. The earlier calmness left a hole in the emptiness. Maybe it was a good time to relax and renew before the next onslaught of cooking.

To my wonder I found this mystery of love transferring itself into the chatter and play going on in the TV room filled now with my family. As I stood at the doorway and gazed in, an organized chaotic exchange of random thoughts and energized conversation buzzed around the room. I chose the rocking chair, planted myself, and entered into the conversation. Everyone talking at once produced a steady hum. Only as my grandson, Davis, tottered on the footstool did a sudden hush come over the group. I went on full alert, his aunt, Christina, spotted him and leaned toward him, while his grandfather made an executive decision and pulled him down, with a gentle reminder that the stool was not a good place for him to be.

This mysterious love morphed from the chaos of paying no attention to closely monitoring an impending situation. The focus shifted from self to the little one who could be in harm's way. This mysterious love had the power to reach into chaos, show its face, and then decide which of us would reach out to divert a fall that could have brought blood, tears, and injury. There hovered over each us a care for the other, but most particularly for the little one whose need for love and attention was the greatest.

I announced to my crowd in the other room that dinner was about ready. Like wasps that smell sweetness, my family appeared in the kitchen. The previously empty space was now full, almost too full. I glanced up, and bodies were everywhere. Clearly everyone hungered for something to eat. The bird came out of the oven. I sliced into it; sure enough, the turkey was not completely done. Disappointment. OK, *just relax; no problem. Stick it back in the oven for a while.* As I slipped the bird back in, my family disappeared, returning to their chatter in the other room. Nothing to do but wait.

What seemed to take hours turned out to be only twenty minutes. I inspected the bird again and pronounced that the meal could proceed. The bustle within the kitchen picked up. Vegetables found their way into serving bowls, the gravy into the microwave, and the wine into glasses on the table. I felt a common goal binding us—the feast of Thanksgiving. When the family crowd had all assembled in the dining room, I found myself once more in the kitchen by myself. Now there was only the chaos of gooey pots and pans. In this mess the mystery of love again appeared. As we prepare to feed one another there is a certain love, a love that takes place around a joyous dinner table. There is love in nourishment: physical, emotional, and spiritual. How badly we all need to be nourished. Here it would be food, but so often the need for nourishment comes from the heart and soul of our very being. Would we find that as well around the Thanksgiving table this year?

A hush fell over the dining room table. My husband yielded the offering of grace to me. In the busyness of all the food preparation, I really hadn't thought about what I was going to say, but the first words came easily: "Loving God, we thank you for the many blessings you have bestowed upon us . . . " My heart and very being overflowed with thanks for all the events of the day. From the smoke cloud in the morning to the now-messy kitchen, I was richly blessed with a family that cared for one another. As the *amen* came out of my mouth, the chatter returned. Each family member has a favorite part of the turkey, and I indulged them in my carving. The competition to see who could eat the most had begun. I watched the plates being piled high with food, and then slowly—and in some cases, not-so-slowly—the food disappeared. After seconds and thirds, there was a collective sigh of contentment around the table for the feast just enjoyed. My son-in-law, Todd, and I got the prize for the cleanest plates. Would there be room for dessert? Of course. When the pies appeared, everyone seemed to have found a second stomach. A little bit of this and a lot of that were squeezed in.

Then dinner was over, finished. My masterpiece was consumed. But the true masterpiece came from the hand of a loving artist. That is the ingredient I had tried desperately to bring to this special day. That is, love, the mysterious spice. With a lot of love, the potatoes were fluffier, and the stuffing held its consistency. With a lot of love even the woody turnips and slightly underdone turkey would nourish body and soul.

As we drifted away from the table and the mess of the kitchen loomed before us, I looked down at my right hand. I could see a battle scar of love. The burn across one knuckle was stark white. *Not good. By morning it will be bright red and the first layer of skin will be gone.* This battle scar of love would be with me for a long time. It would take care and nursing to restore the skin. It hurts and is unsightly, but the scar would be a reminder of an evening filled with blessings and love. There is a great mystery in love.

TWENTY-ONE

The Pastor

"The life was the light of all people."
John 1:4

I t is Sunday. I have just left church. As I drive home, my mind starts to wander, and I think of Dr. Webster. After more than fifty years, Dr. Webster remains in my heart as if just yesterday. Dr. Webster first brought me close to God.

The white church stood atop a hill with a wonderful sledding lawn out front. From the top to the bottom, sledders found the most awesome ride when the snow was just right and had been packed down for maximum speed. I often thought about those rides when I went to church on Sunday mornings. It seemed appropriate that we should climb a hill to encounter God. The large pillars out front welcomed us into the church building. The inside of the sanctuary was white with dark wood trim on the pews, a simple place with no stained-glass windows or ornamentation on the walls or ceiling. As we walked into the sanctuary, the altar stood in front of us down a long center aisle carpeted in red. A cross hung on the back wall, seemingly suspended in midair. To the left was the lectern and to the right the pulpit. On Sundays, the sanctuary was filled to overflowing with parishioners almost every week. We always found a spot on the left-hand side toward the back.

Attendance at Sunday school was expected, and so, throughout my younger years, halfway through the worship service all the children were dismissed to go to their classes. With the others, I filed into the attached building for the lesson of the day. I was secretly delighted when I went through confirmation and joined the church, because that meant no more Sunday school. I didn't have anything against it, but I had reached the age at which I preferred to stay in church and listen to the sermon. And that was because of Dr. Webster.

Every preacher has his or her own style. Dr. Webster had several unique styles. First was his wardrobe. He wore the traditional white clerical collar but the kind that had two white rectangles hanging from it. They looked like two long front teeth extending from his neck. It was intriguing because of being so different and distinguished. He didn't wear a clergy stole but rather a stately academic hood over his neck that hung down the back of his black robe. The red velvet lining of the hood was lush and eye-catching for a young person, as were the red velvet bars on the blousy sleeves of his robe. He wore his robe with a certain authority. As he moved around the altar, his robe flowed this way and that with each turn and gesture. Those were the times when the church pulpit commanded a certain power, and Dr. Webster fulfilled that image. As a young person I looked up to my minister, but more than that, I came to know him as a messenger of God's Word. When Dr. Webster took his place in the pulpit, you could hear a pin drop in the sanctuary. All minds and hearts turned to him and his message. The worship space was filled with a holy hush.

Dr. Webster spoke with a marvelous Scottish brogue. The words rolled off his tongue. His accent captivated me. Words carried their very essence and feeling. The amazing thing about Dr. Webster's brogue was that it kept me hanging on and listening carefully to his message. I have come to believe that this was God's gift to him, because I knew everyone in the sanctuary attended intently to his sermon. As I listened I heard the message from beginning to end—from the heart.

Ponder the question of listening and hearing. How often do we listen but not hear? Words tumble out of a person's mouth, and we often drift away, not truly hearing or comprehending what is being said; or we find ourselves thinking more about what we are going to say next. We are ready with the reply before the last word comes out of the other person's mouth. Did we truly hear? Maybe, maybe not. When I reflect back on Dr. Webster's sermons, I remember coming away from his sermons thinking, or changed, or moved—something was different. I believe his message touched me, because I was not only listening, but hearing. I feel I truly heard the Word through this man's heart.

But not just his speaking moved me. Here I witnessed a man so passionate about his message and the gospel that, at times, it brought him to tears. He would start slowly, building a background for his message. Then he would move to a place so real and so moving for him that tears would come. He would look out on the assembled congregation, lean on the pulpit, put his finger to his lips, and pause to try to catch his emotions. At the height of the message he often could not. His voice trembled, his mouth curled down, and I glimpsed wetness around his eyes. In essence he was asking us, Did you really understand the power in God's Word? Can you feel the emotion of the gospel? Are you filled with the passion of Jesus Christ? Will you dare walk this road with me, a road that may even bring us to tears?

As I sat and listened, very often a beam of sunlight would float through the eastern window and warm my face. Even to this day, as I feel sunlight on my face, I often recall how this moment in church had such power. "What has come into being in him was life, and the life was the light of all people. The light shines in the darkness, and the darkness did not overcome it" (John 1:3–5). Darkness cannot overcome the light.

Over the years of hearing Dr. Webster's sermons, I came to believe that here was the presence of Christ in the light of this place and time reaching out to the assembled people. Here was one man reaching out to his congregation with the good news, so powerful that his heart would melt into tears of joy. If everyone present on Sunday mornings felt as I did, I'm not surprised that our church grew under Dr. Webster's pastorate and that his congregants were transformed into Christians led and nurtured by the Word.

Like so many young people who go off to college and leave their hometown, I left my church and Dr. Webster behind. I left Dr. Webster before the years of the Vietnam War, hippies, and the "God is dead" movement. But not really. He and his passion for God's Word must have stayed with me—not on a front burner but on a back one. He was in my heart more than I realized at the time. And then, following college, Dr. Webster came physically into my life again when he officiated at my wedding before he left for a new home. Our marriage vows—one last blessing for me and my new life.

What became of the church upon his departure? The church has continued to grow over the years under succeeding pastors, which is good because a church needs to be more than just the pastor. Many people have worshiped and praised in that church in which I grew up. The sanctuary is much bigger. My sledding hill was cut into to build a parking lot to accommodate all the cars. The choirs, Sunday school, and mission programs continue to flourish and grow. I have attended the church only a few times since I was married there in 1971, and in a grace-filled way, Dr. Webster remains there for me.

Thirty-some years later, Dr. Webster entered my life once more. Not physically this time but spiritually. I felt a calling to go to seminary. In the admissions process I had to write a paper on the spiritual journey that had led me to this decision. My paper began with Dr. Webster. It began with the passion I had caught for the gospel of Jesus Christ and for the love of God that Dr. Webster had instilled in me. Through my young adult years I often would wonder what I would do with that passion. Little did I know what God had in store for me. The call was now to seminary. I knew in my heart that Dr. Webster's passion would go with me.

TWENTY-TWO

The Couch

"I am with you always."
Matthew 28:20

Are couches for sitting or for lying on? That depends. My preference has always been to lie on them, because I've always thought of a couch as an informal, relaxed place. A couch is where I put my body when it is hard to sit up but easy to recline. Sitting on a couch has its merits, but when I see a couch, I always size it up for how it would feel to lie on it. What this says is I have spent a lot of time lying on the couches in the places I've called home. It is my preference.

And so, finding me relaxing and reading on my couch after work this afternoon in 1972 was not unusual. The couch of which I speak is a great couch—a true young adult's, 1970s couch. Bright orange, this couch was not for everybody. (I still have it in my basement, unable to part with it.) The high back prevented me from having to slouch to rest my head; I merely leaned back comfortably. The armrest stood high enough to elevate my head at an appropriate angle for reading while lying down. A pillow helped to make the couch the ideal place to relax after a long day of teaching.

I reflect on a particular afternoon as I reclined on my orange couch. The day had been calm and unremarkable, but even so, the couch beckoned me to come and stretch out. I gave in. I lay there comfortably reading a magazine. Suddenly

I began to feel my heart beating. Of course it was beating. But why should it be pounding when I was just lying there on the couch? This sensation came without warning. It came out of nowhere. At first I chose to ignore it. No big deal. I took a couple of big breaths. It did no good. My heart continued to beat really hard. My heart then began to "flip" around, missing a beat and then a beat too many. I lay there trying my hardest to relax. I was convinced it was just momentary and would stop with the next breath, yet it continued. Before I understood what was really happening, my life had changed forever.

Was I sick? How sick could I be? How could anything be wrong with my heart? I had always been very athletic. There just couldn't be anything wrong. As my heart continued to flip around, I kept telling myself there just couldn't be anything wrong. No way. But after a half an hour or longer of this I started to get scared that something was truly wrong. I lay there by myself. My husband was not due to be home for another hour. I was scared to get up. I was scared to try to get to the phone. If I passed out when I rose from the couch, that wouldn't be good. If I was conscious, I could at least tell someone what was going on. And so I lay on the couch growing more and more frightened.

A piece of me screamed, *this isn't happening to me. I do not understand this. How can it be?* I found myself drowning in disbelief. Every gasp for air proved futile because I just couldn't calm my pounding heart. My head bobbed above the waters of disbelief, but how long could it remain there? I could not control "this thing" that had invaded my body. It had a life of its own and was slowly consuming mine. Why? Why? I was alone with no one to answer that question.

Have you ever felt alone? Truly alone? I felt really alone that afternoon. I was here, and the rest of the world went about their day not knowing I lay on the couch scared and sick.

Our cottage was situated on a large estate, so all that surrounded me were trees and lawn, a long driveway, and the street at a distance. Who would hear me if I called out? No one. I heard no cars go by. I was alone. What I felt was a darkness, a darkness that seemed to envelop the room. As the trees cast their shadows on the cottage, they stood cold and dark. The sun faded and the afternoon light slowly began to slip away. The light was leaving me. As the darkness closed in on the room, I felt even more alone. And as the light faded toward night, my inner being also darkened, casting away the warmth of life.

The wisdom in the book of Ecclesiastes read, "For if they fall, one will lift up the other; but woe to one who is alone and falls and does not have another to help. Again, if two lie together, they keep warm; but how can one keep warm alone?" (Ecclesiastes 4:10–11). How can we keep warm alone? I felt alone, cold, and helpless that afternoon.

I continued to wonder when my husband would arrive home. He could walk through the door at some point, but would it be soon enough? *I could call him on the phone.* I lay on the couch contemplating that move. It felt like the smart thing to do, but a little voice in my head said again, *don't get up off this couch. Stay where you are. Remember you might pass out, and you'll end up on the floor unable to communicate with your husband when he does get home.* My heart pounded and flipped around. No matter how I breathed or moved, it continued. Time stood still. I watched the hands of my watch move at a dead crawl toward six o'clock. Surely my husband would be home by then.

That afternoon dragged endlessly. Time remained stuck in the scariness of the moment. My heart continued to pound. That awareness was the only reality available to me.

Finally, the six o'clock hour arrived, and I heard the door open. My husband called my name. I called back that I was here lying on the couch, please come and help.

"What's wrong?" were his first words. I was a healthy, athletic teacher; what was I doing lying on the couch calling out for help? In desperation I tried to explain what had happened and what was happening now. He stood in disbelief. He understood it no better than I did. His expression displayed puzzlement. This was unknown territory for both of us. This uncertainty scared us both the most. The unknown. We can deal with what we know about, but what we don't know is unsettling and fearful.

I continued, trying to explain my symptoms to him. This dialogue went on for some time. Eventually, we came to the realization that we should head to a doctor, now. We called a doctor and learned we should, in fact, come right over. The urgency in the doctor's voice unsettled us. Even so, I was reluctant to get up off the couch, but I had to. Instead of standing still, time now raced away from me. On my husband's arm, I walked slowly into the darkness of the night. The events of that afternoon changed my life forever. In spite of all this, I am amazed that I still enjoy lying on a couch.

As I reflect back on that afternoon, it gives me pause to think about the conflicting emotions that went through my head and heart. To be in denial, to know the unknown, and to be alone all deserve a closer look. Could I put some kind of face on that afternoon that was recognizable?

Life is a journey. Up until that afternoon I saw myself walking in the sunshine of life. I had received a fine education and now had the job of my choice and a loving husband. I was young and my life's journey stretched out before me with much to be thankful for. I had had the opportunity to smell the richness of the flowers along the way. The lush green grass had tickled my toes and surrounding trees had stood above me in all their beauty. This was my path until that afternoon when I found myself falling into a deep, dark hole. I had not seen it coming. Had it been there all the time, lurking in the shadows? I most certainly would have gone around the hole if possible, but before I knew it, I was falling. Falling into this dark hole.

What does the hole look like? I believe, metaphorically, each hole in life has its own shape and character. This hole is just big enough around that as I fall, I can stretch out my arms and my fingers are within inches of the sides. That's not much of a diameter. There is no bottom, and I am suspended in this abyss. It is damp and very dark except for the light shining in from above. The light is bright but streaming in like a tunnel, present but seemingly unreachable. The walls confine my body, every thought, and any spirit I can muster. The dirt walls are dotted with stones, and as I touch the walls, small pieces of dirt and pebbles fall downward past me. I never hear them hit bottom. There is no bottom in this hole. The loosened pieces descend into a nothingness, like pieces of my life falling away to a place I will never know again.

In this place the unknown surrounds me and begins to suck the life out of me. It is a strange place. It is a place I have never been before. It is a place that has no end. It is a place that confines. It is a place where my life is suspended in a vacuum. It is a place where every ounce of control has been drained away from me. It is a place from which I am convinced I will not be able to get out. The walls feel like they are closing in and the light dims. My only thought is: *this can't be happening to me. This is unreal. I cannot and will not accept this place.* I try to push the sense of reality away and keep it at a distance, but I cannot. The dirt and darkness are there. The hole in life's journey is there. These things can't be denied. The walls close in, and it is only me alone in this hole of life.

Aloneness. Do we fall into it? Do we seek it? Can it be thrust upon us? By our very choices do we end up alone? Is being alone a good thing or a bad thing? Is being alone a difficult thing? How does aloneness affect our very being? I believe it can and it does. To fall into a hole that closes out the world and forces us to be alone is one of the most difficult paths we walk in life's journey. My situation afforded me no choice. I was alone, all by myself, lying on my orange couch. Never in my life had I felt so alone.

Each of us has felt alone at some point in our life. It is a state that carries with it mixed emotions from isolation and fear to renewal and relaxation. On this particular afternoon I was overcome with fear as my heart pounded in my chest and I lay waiting alone for my husband. It was a scary, dark feeling, and yet in reflection over the years since this incident, I have reveled in the opportunity to be alone to refresh my mind and spirit—to get away from it all and just listen, think, empty myself, and pray. I cherished those opportunities when I chose to walk on the beach alone, or in a garden to revel in the color and fragrances. To be alone. Again I ponder, life is curious, how a state of being can be at one time a curse and another a blessing?

But are we ever truly alone? I have come to more fully believe and appreciate that I am not. Whether I am in a crowd, or challenged by life-changing health issues, or walking on the beach by myself, I am not alone. My faith has grown as I have confronted the realities of life. I believe that God is there. Jesus walks besides me. The Holy Spirit guides. My faith was less than mature when I lay on the couch that afternoon with my heart flipping around. I didn't know the power of prayer. Was I even thinking about God that afternoon? No. With all the "church" I had been exposed to and the passionate sermons I had heard, I didn't even think to turn to God to calm the ever-increasing sense of doubt and fear. As I reflect back on that afternoon, this is a real sadness of that moment. I endured that scary time alone and didn't have to. I was consumed by the darkness and depth of the hole instead of looking to the light coming in from above. As the psalmist wrote, "Bless the LORD, O my soul, who redeems your life from the Pit, who crowns you with steadfast love and mercy" (Psalm 103:2, 4). Here is the light that shines from above into the holes of our lives. We need to keep our faces turned toward that light so our hearts may be filled with love and mercy. I know that now, but did not then.

I was *scared stiff* that afternoon. I was scared of the darkness that had befallen me without explanation. I was scared of the unknown. This forbidding hole, this deep dark hole in life. Both in mind and heart, I rationalize that I can't possibly know everything there is to know about every situation that I might confront in my lifetime. But the fear of the moment squashed all the comprehension I could muster. A little piece of me fought for the former self, but the reality of the situation was so real as to be unreal. Was this a dream from which I would awake? Yes, it was. No, it was not. Denial kept alive the possibility of awakening from this dream. But it was not a dream. It was a real "pit" of life.

There would be more "pits" along the way, ultimately helping to form the new self from the former. From each success in climbing toward the light and not being sucked toward the bottomless dark hole, I have gained the strength to live the life that lies before me, always with God's help. As I have learned, life's journey is not easy. It has been hard work many a time, but there is the promise of Christ that holds me in a close relationship to God: "And remember, I am with you always, even to the end of the age" (Matthew 28:20).

My life changed that afternoon as I lay on my orange couch. One of the many blessings I have come to experience over the years because of that time is that the light does shine from above and with it comes a love with the power to overcome the darkest and deepest holes in life. "The LORD is my light and my salvation; whom shall I fear? The LORD is the stronghold of my life; of whom shall I be afraid?" (Psalm 27:1).

TWENTY-THREE

The Wreath

"She gave birth to her firstborn son."
Luke 2:7

The freshly cut evergreens formed a circle. The three purple and one pink candle rose stately from the greens. The one short, fat white candle held its place of honor in the center. Such was the Advent wreath my mother used to make for the Advent and Christmas seasons. It found its place in the living room, as a reminder of why we were celebrating and what we were celebrating. Much to my mother's credit, she would gather the family around the Advent wreath each of the Sundays preceding Christmas Day. We weren't always willing to participate. Yet she would persevere, and so on Sunday afternoons we found ourselves in the living room before the greens and candles.

From the church, she had obtained a series of readings for each Sunday in Advent. This was the guide for our service at home. We would take turns reading the Scriptures for the week. As a child it seemed "dry," that is, until we got to the singing part. One of my fondest memories is the gusto with which my father used to sing the hymn of the week. In his beautiful low voice he would lead the singing, belting out the words. Clearly, this was the part Dad enjoyed most, as evidenced by the increased volume and tone of his voice. Many a time we kids would end up with a case of the giggles because Dad sang so loudly, but that didn't deter him a bit. Though the laughter seemed a bit sacrilegious, that singing kept the time of our Advent together as a family fresh within my mind and heart over the years. Even today we laugh about Dad singing so loudly.

Over the years, the messages of the Advent wreath have come to shape my thoughts surrounding the Christmas season. The greens and candles brought forth more fully the real meaning of Christmas. It is about the light brought into the world through the birth of a baby, not about the tinsel and toys. With the lighting of each candle I am reminded first of hope, then peace and love, and, on the last Sunday, of joy. The light of the candles brings the light of each of these blessings to the forefront of my thoughts and all that I seek along my faith journey.

On the first Sunday, we lit a candle to proclaim the coming of the light of God into the world. In this light there is *hope,* and so because of Christ, we believe that good is stronger than evil and that God wants us to work for good in the world. The coming of hope has grown into a powerful meaning of Christmas for me. The Advent liturgy speaks of a larger hope for the world, but hope needs to come down to dwell in each one of us. I believe God does call each of us in our own way to work for good in our world. To work for good in our larger world, but also to work for good in the smaller, more subtle things. This is the world we participate in daily, and over which we may have some control because of the choices we make.

I have been blessed with so much over the years, not only a wonderful family and friends but material things as well. At Christmas we kids often received the toys we'd asked for. Wishes came true, and the magic of Christmas gave us many hours of playtime. Mother and Dad, grandmothers and grandfathers, showered us with wonderful gifts. I give thanks for their generosity and love for me as a child.

When my children came along, I followed in my parents' footsteps. Buying "things" for my children at Christmas gave me the greatest pleasure. The expressions on their faces on Christmas morning when they opened their gifts are to be cherished always. I felt so blessed that I had the wherewithal to give in such a way. Like many families with children, the toys of Christmas multiplied very quickly. We quickly found our family room overcome with toys of all shapes, sizes, and colors.

At some point I said to myself, this is just too much. I don't remember when or why. It might have been appeals at Christmastime from organizations like Toys for Tots or the Salvation Army. My children had so much and there were children who had little or nothing. My children would know the fun of packages under the Christmas tree, but too many other children would not know that happiness. We could help. We would help. This would be a very valuable lesson for my children, but I, too, could learn from what we were about to do.

I asked each of my children to select two of their toys that they wished to give to a child less fortunate than themselves. It needed to be in good condition, in what we now term "gently used." They asked how they were to choose, since they loved all their toys. I told them if they had enjoyed it, chances are this toy could continue bringing joy, but to another child. I was surprised, and they were too, that it wasn't hard to choose which toys they wanted to pass along. In a couple of cases, I remember one of my children saying that they had really liked this particular toy and were hoping that whoever ended up with it would too. After all toys had been selected, we drove over to the distribution center together so my children could give their toys away in person. I believe we all felt good on the drive home.

In giving there is hope. In giving of the self, a hope can be born in both the recipient and giver. In our own small or larger ways, God calls us to work for good in our world. This is the hope born into our world at Christmastime. So, to learn the lesson of giving for another's benefit is to take in the hope of a better world where good is indeed stronger than evil.

On the second Sunday, with the coming of the light of the next candle, there is *peace*. Christ is called the "Prince of Peace." Christ's name is Emmanuel, which means "God with us." With this light we are promised the presence of Christ-with-us offering us peace each day.

As with hope, our world has a desperate need for peace. Around the world people pray for peace for those places torn apart by hatred, violence, and killing. Prayer feels so fruitless at times. We are so small and the problems so great. How can praying for peace possibly help? I have no answer to that question. All I can state is that over the years, as my faith has matured, I feel my prayers for peace in the larger world are being heard. It is one of those mysteries of faith that I embrace and try not to question; I am reassured by the promise of Christ that if I pray my prayers will be heard.

To know the presence of Christ day by day I think is very difficult at Christmastime. Why? Because society bombards us with both great poverty and the glitter of materialism. If you doubt that, recall your last trip to a mall the weeks after Thanksgiving.

Two weeks before Christmas I circled the parking lot one more time in hope that a space would become available. Cars jockeyed for position. Some drivers were so rude as to cut right in front of me as I waited for a car to back out of a parking space. Under my breath I steamed, *that space was mine!* I finally found a space, but as luck would have it, the space was at the far end of the parking lot. I got out, bundled up, and moved through the cold air as fast as I could. The mall was packed with shoppers. As I walked about, I saw person after person with large shopping bags. Everyone appeared tense and programmed. They were here to buy gifts for all the people on their very long shopping list. Buy something and move on to the next. Buy that and move on to another store.

I picked my way through the maze of people. No luck in the first store. On to the next to find the perfect gift for my daughter. Success. I found *the gift* and went to pay for it. At the cash register, I looked at the faces of the people standing in line. Most suggested an annoyance that the whole process was taking far too long. I must admit the faces depicted how I felt inside. I was no different. I wanted to be done with all this shopping and move on. Time was of the essence. Too much to do and not enough time to get it all done. Store upon store tried to lure me in to make a purchase. So many "things" to buy, to add to all the "stuff" we already have. Our materialistic society runs contrary to the peace we seek for ourselves as we journey the road of life. We battle materialism at every corner.

Christmas lights and elegant displays fill our lives at Christmastime with glitter and tinsel. As I passed one store, I was struck by the cute ornaments. They were displayed on a beautifully decorated Christmas tree. In all their glitter they were very enticing. I held up one ornament after another. They were all so cute, how could I choose? I looked through the bins and racks of ornaments before I decided not to buy anything. Don't know why. Something stopped me. Perhaps I realized that I already had enough perfectly fine ornaments for the tree. Perhaps I realized they were more expensive that I would have liked. Perhaps my struggling under a load of shopping bags made me hesitant to carry another one. Perhaps I found it within myself to not get sucked in by the tinsel and glitter of the season. Where was the peace in all this? It certainly was not with me that day.

I have come to believe that peace is difficult to find during the Christmas season because of "the want" that overtakes us. Our world is constantly asking us what we want. Do we want that, do we want this? The frequently asked question at Christmas is *what do you want?* As we think more and more about what we want, we lose the notion of what we need. There are times in my life when I have run headlong into places and people who have a real need. I go around asking people what they want for Christmas when there are so many people in need. Identifying some of those needs has been a quest of mine in recent years. It hasn't always been easy or on the forefront of my mind, but I am seeking to be more intentional about keeping my eyes and ears open for ways I can help. When I stop and pray, I often feel an unsettledness over the magnitude of the problems and realize how little I can really help. In the "wants," little peace exists.

In those weeks between Thanksgiving and Christmas, as we light the Advent candles, I struggle to find an inner peace, the presence of Christ that can bring serenity. Have you ever wished you could have five more hours in the day in the time before Christmas? Life is just plain and simply hectic. I wished I could slow down and rest in the peace that had been promised. Wouldn't that be an awesome way to prepare for the birth of Jesus? To push aside the busyness and commercialism and move into a peace of mind and heart that both renews and restores. Emmanuel is born to us. *God with us* comes into our world. Oh, that I could invite God into my world day by day and so know more fully the peace of Christmas.

On the third Sunday the candle is love. With the coming of God's light into the world there is *love*. This great love helps us to love God and one another. Love is the umbrella for me. Under love I find hope. Under love I find peace. Under love I find joy. Under love I find I can give of myself to those around me and beyond. Under love is where I find God, our God who loves us unconditionally. This is the God who had such a great love for us that He sent

His only Son into the world as a baby. Through that birth I know an omnipresent love, and so, too, forgiveness and reconciliation.

I always feel love in the air during the Christmas season. It can be hard to find amid the busyness and commercialism of the season, but it is there. At times I need to look hard for it, and other times it seems to hit me over the head and say, "Here I am, do you see me?" I am entering the store, and in front of me I see a woman holding the door for the young mother with a carriage and packages in hand. I am riding the subway, and I see a young man hop quickly out of his seat for an elderly gentleman. I go through a tollbooth, and the operator smiles and wishes me a good day.

I recall one particular day when I was blessed by the gift of love from a stranger. A big treat during Christmas at my grandparent's house in New Orleans was to go to the zoo. One of the largest "cages" was the monkey's house and island with a moat around it. There was a large rock in the center with lots of gym equipment on which the monkeys played. The monkeys would even occasionally go for a swim to get closer to the people. A little store near the entrance sold popcorn and peanuts. Granny always treated us—my brother, sister, and me—to both. The bag of popcorn was our treat, and the peanuts were for the monkeys. We stood at the rail and threw the peanuts to the monkeys. Needless to say, we went through the small bag of peanuts fairly quickly. I wasn't a very good shot or strong enough to get the peanuts to the island all the time, but I would keep on throwing anyway.

Soon my bag was empty and so was my sister's. No more peanuts to throw to keep the show going. My sister and I watched covertly as my brother continued to hurl peanuts at the monkeys. We were sad we had no more peanuts. It must have shown on our faces, because the woman standing next to my little sister approached her. She handed my sister her bag of peanuts and said, you were having so much fun, please take mine. My sister was ecstatic. More peanuts. More fun. With a hasty thanks, the game started all over again. It's funny the things we remember. Such a simple thing, yet that woman's thoughtfulness for a little girl left a lasting impression on this now-grown woman. It is the gift of sharing, of caring, of seeing another and passing along the love you have to give. This is a piece of the love of Christmas.

I often fantasize what a true blessing it would be if every gift given at Christmas carried the love of Christ in the selection and the giving. The number of gifts given wouldn't be nearly as important as the love put into the giving. Perhaps this is why I've always treasured the handmade gifts I've received. Perhaps this is why, after all these years, I still have all the handmade Christmas ornaments my children made in preschool. They are crude, but cute. They are now faded and some have pieces broken off, but every year I treasure them as I remove them from the Christmas box. I smile. Not too many find their way to the Christmas tree anymore. Their joy is now in the memories they bring back. The angels, which are made of pine cones and milkweed pods, are the one exception. Each year I find them carefully wrapped in tissue paper. These angels were made by my children when they were in nursery school. Each is distinctive and charming in its simplicity. Carefully, I place them on the sideboard in the dining room. Invariably there is a wing that has to be stuck back on, but they take their place of honor every year. My choir of angels singing of the love of Christmas.

On the fourth Sunday, a candle is lit amongst the giggles over Dad's loud singing. With this light there is *joy*—joy that is ours not only at Christmas, but always. As I journey along the path of faith, I have come to distinguish the difference between happiness and joy. Happiness is a state of mind, an emotional state brought to the forefront by circumstances or another person. As we interact one with another, we can bring forth happiness and feel good inside. To know happiness is a gift of life. To know joy, I believe, is the greater gift. To know the state of joy is to be gifted with something far greater. I have come to believe that to know joy is to know a certain holiness. Joy is infused with the divine will. It is God's greatest pleasure for us. To know joy at the Advent season is to bring us closer to the birth of Jesus. To know joy is to know God.

As I walked around the farm stand, I kept my eye out for the Christmas tree for this year. I carefully studied the selections. Some were too small, others not full enough, some too big, this one, the wrong variety. Like most of us, I have purchased many Christmas trees over the years. I recall the year we were going away so I bought a tiny tree. It must have been the top of a much taller one. It found its place of honor on a table in front of a window; it had only one strand of lights on it. It created the most wonderful illusion.

From the street it looked like we had a gigantic tree. The year my son announced his engagement, I went and bought the biggest tree we could fit in the house.

Over the years we shared in the joy of my mother's Christmas trees, which she decorated with live candles. On Christmas Day we'd light the candles with one of us standing by holding a fire extinguisher. Just in case. One year we bought a live Christmas tree to plant on our property after the season. And then there was the tree that lost almost all of its needles before Christmas Day. What a disaster. Most recently, I had the tree I bought delivered and set up by the people from whom I bought it. Now that's a living joy.

The greens of Christmas have taken on more meaning for me. Yes, my trees bring back fond memories, but it is the presence of God's good creation within the house that has brought greater joy for me. There is something wonderful about fresh greens, like my mother's fresh greens in the Advent wreath years ago. They are a symbol of life. They are a symbol of our earth. They are *ever green,* a symbol of the beauty and freshness of life itself—a symbol of the joy that is found in Christmas. The green of nature has a holiness about it. It symbolizes creation. It symbolizes the birth and rebirth of God's creation and elicits a state of joy. May the joy we feel at Christmas resonate with the holiness of God's divine will to bring a savior into our midst. This is joy.

The thick white candle at the center of the Advent wreath was lit on Christmas Eve. The Christ candle took its place of honor and holiness at the evening service. For the last thirty years I have attended my church's eleven o'clock Christmas Eve service. Before the service the congregants are given small white candles to be lit at the close of the service. The light is taken from the Christ candle at the center of the Advent wreath and passed among the congregation until there is a sea of light.

One Christmas Eve in the late '90s was bitterly cold. We had had more than a foot of snow a few days before. The bright moonlight reflected off the new snow. It was a true classic white New England Christmas. People filled the sanctuary. As we began to sing "Silent Night," we proceeded out of the sanctuary into the garden between the church and the fellowship hall. A stream of lights moved rhythmically with the music. The deep snow buried the garden, but the pathways through the garden had been shoveled.

With the others I walked along the path lined with a bank of snow on either side. With the snow knee-deep in front of us, we stood in a large circle. The light of the candles was incredibly beautiful reflecting off the snow. The moon and stars above and the lights from the Christ candle below set the Christmas Eve scene. As we sang I could see my breath in the cold air. This breath of life floated around the circle. Holiness overtook me and the power of the moment filled my very being. In this light I knew the hope, peace, love, and joy of Christ. For me this is what Christmas is all about.

TWENTY-FOUR

The Least

"As you did it to one of the least of these"
Matthew 25:40

The little white figure signaling "walk" flashed on and off, telling me I could cross the city street safely. A cold breeze prompted me to pull my scarf up around my chin and scrunch down into my coat for warmth. I crossed the street, hurried down the stairs, and pulled open the door that showed its age along the edges from wear and tear. The warm air felt good as it hit my face. In the large room, tables were lined up like large dominos. A few women sat here and there. These women came to this place for many reasons, but most particularly for a free, hot, freshly cooked luncheon meal. Some talked together, others read, and others sat staring at the cup of coffee in front of them. They looked tired and worn. Here I was witness to just a sampling of the homeless women of the city of Boston. The world had not been kind to these women for a variety of reasons. As I went by each table, I couldn't help but wonder about their stories. How would I feel as they told it? I found myself overtaken by a sense of curiosity as well as by sadness. Had God let these women down? Had my God forsaken them? What had they done that landed them here in a soup kitchen?

The shelter's kitchen felt even warmer than the dining room. Lunch was cooking, the dishwasher was running, and the volunteers were hustling about preparing lunch. Why was I here? To wash the pots and pans. Not a glamorous role, but one that many who volunteered at the shelter didn't want to do. For some unknown reason I enjoyed this task, perhaps because of the simplicity of it, but more importantly, I could see immediate accomplishment. There are so many things we do in life in which no results can be seen, where what we have done drifts into thin air, or does not yield results for many years. Here in this kitchen, just the opposite occurred—the pan was dirty, now the pan was clean.

How often have we each struggled with settling an emotion running wild in our hearts? How often have we struggled with a problem that seemed to almost cause our minds to implode? All those intangibles of life can cause us much unsettledness. We pine and worry, fuss and calculate, and the answers elude us. In these moments we are even so bold as to ask God, "Where are you? Why won't you help me figure out what to do?" And sadly, as we hurry about trying to solve our problem, we fail to stop and listen for that voice. Maybe the answer was there, and we just hurried by it to get somewhere else. I likened this to the pot I was trying to wash but couldn't get clean. And so here at this lunch place, washing pots and seeing them clean becomes very therapeutic. I can see that I have made a difference. Dirty, clean.

After lunch has been served, the pots grow in number, and the task grows tiring. Strangely, that weariness almost feels good. I have found out through the years that hard work has never hurt me. A sense of accomplishment begins to take hold. When the last pot has been washed, the task is complete. When I am done, I know I am done. That is that. There is a certain finality to it all. The finality feels good. I have finished the task and can see the results shine before me. Not so in all tasks.

After I left the kitchen, I wandered out again among the remaining women who were probably not looking forward to going back out on the cold street to live out the rest of their day. A sense of sorrow hit me. I wondered what the night would hold for them. As I left the building, I was warm from the pot washing, so when the cold air struck my face, this time it felt good. The briskness of it refreshed and rejuvenated my body and my spirit. I hurried up the street to run an errand. In and out of the store in just a short time, and I was back on the street, back to the train station. By this time I'd cooled off from my work, and the icy breeze began to chill me. My clothes were damp from hard work and splashing water, so I picked up my pace to get back inside as soon as possible.

The women at the lunch place stayed with me that day, as they usually do. They had been filled, literally, until they found their next meal. I, too, was filled with the certain satisfaction of knowing that in some small way I had helped a woman who was down-and-out. I prayed that in some small way, through my presence, she felt someone cared and loved her in the true biblical sense. To say I felt good sounds so trite. I ask myself what is that feeling, that good feeling like, really? It is hard to put into words, but I suspect we have all tasted that emotion at some point. How to describe it? I was tired, but my steps felt lighter. I was cold, but my heart felt warm. I was hurrying, but time seemed to stand still in the joy of that moment. The joy that I had done just a little something to make this world a better place for someone filled me. I was in that frame of heart when God touched me again.

As I made my way to the corner, I noticed two mothers, each pushing a baby carriage. They were engaged in an animated conversation. The babies were quiet, enjoying the ride. The mothers were loaded down and heading for the store directly in front of me. As they approached the store, they began to jockey for position. Finally, the first mother held the door for the second mother. Their carriages were so big it took a bit of a juggling act for the first mother to hold the heavy door and her carriage simultaneously, but she managed. The second mother got herself inside and then turned to help her friend. This portended to be a difficult maneuver. As I watched this quickly unfold, I found myself running up to the door of the store and holding it open for the second mother. The door was heavy, but easy for me to hold because I was empty-handed. Without a word, we took our places. One mother stood inside. The other started up the stairs, and I held the door open. As the second mother fumbled up the steps and into the store, she turned to me with a smile and offered me a very sincere, "thank you."

I read in her face both a sense of surprise and of relief. The words she spoke felt so genuine to me. I sensed that the way the words came out surprised her. Perhaps she had not initially realized how much she really appreciated the gesture, but as she went through the door thankfulness overtook her. As it did me. In that moment we made a connection. A simple smile, a simple gesture had been offered and received. How we yearn for connection in today's world. If we keep ourselves open, it does happen.

To this day that mother's face remains in my mind's eye. Her eyes were young and bright. Her body language told me I had made life a little easier for her. I was touched by her reaction to my gesture. I thought to myself, *I have just spent two hours washing pots and pans trying to make a difference in someone's life, and here, in a matter of seconds, I've done just that.* As I walked away I pondered the words of Jesus: "And when was it that we saw you a stranger and welcomed you, or naked and gave you clothing? . . . Truly I tell you, just as you did it to one of the least of these who are members of my family, you did it to me" (Matthew 25:38, 40). It is not a matter of time; it is a matter of the heart. Whether it is two hours, five years, or just the flash of a moment, caring matters. From the largest to the smallest gesture, a hand held out in love is a morsel of compassion. If we think it otherwise, we are losing out on many an opportunity. My lifetime is made up of years, minutes, and seconds, and each contributes to the whole of living and loving.

Do we rush down streets with our heads down, living only in our own little worlds, our own little moments? Are our minds and hearts closed to the little needs around us? I get sucked into that trap probably more often than I would like to admit. It is easy to do. Can a simple act and a smile turn us around, turn our hearts around? I believe so. This is God's gift to us. The question is, "Have you opened that gift today?"

TWENTY-FIVE

The Clutter

"For theirs is the kingdom of heaven."
Matthew 5:3

One more thing to take to the attic. I opened the door and surveyed the large room, taking in all the "stuff." There were piles of household items from my daughter Christina, baby things from my daughter Elizabeth, books, old out-of-date athletic equipment, and just a lot of other "things" that had found their way into the attic. As I added the newest items to the collection, I left thinking, *what a lot of clutter!*

Clutter has become a part of our lives. Maybe it has always been that way, but in today's world, where we have so much, all those "things" never seem to leave the house. The stuff goes up (to the attic) or down (to the basement) but never out (of the house). Why do we save all these things anyway? I don't believe any of us enjoys the clutter surrounding us, but who knows if we may need that "thing" at some point in the future, and so we store it someplace. I guess some of us are just pack rats by nature, while others are not. Will I ever ski again? Probably not, and if I did, certainly the skis in the attic would be so old as to be unsafe. So why do they continue to lean against the wall up there? Why have I not taken the time or interest in getting rid of them in some appropriate manner? They are cluttering up the attic. Just because I have the space doesn't mean I have to fill the space.

In reflection, clutter affects our lives. We laugh about how we can barely see the furnace in the basement over our mounds of stuff, but we don't want to admit that all it creates is chaos. An unsettledness overtakes us, and life just feels more chaotic. Who of us needs more chaos in our lives? Our minds are already full of schedules, appointments, chores to do, and paperwork or computer work with which to contend. With some kind of order, we are challenged to keep our lives from disarray. Some of us do it with lists, some with tickler files, and others by memory alone. Either way, clutter makes maintaining order more difficult. And so, as our physical lives fill with clutter, we are mentally challenged to keep it all straight. It is no wonder that many of us are exhausted.

Clutter, too, has a way of permeating our emotional lives. It brings us to the edge. A frustration sets in. "Why can't I keep it all straight?" we ask ourselves. "Why can't I remember what to do next or what needs to be done first?" Thanks to the clutter of this world all around us, we grow frustrated at our lack of control. It eats at us. It unsettles us. But is it truly due to a lack of control? We are individuals. We have been taught to be individuals. We have been taught to seek control of our world. Lack of control scares us. But again, is clutter out of our control?

What we need to remember is each of us chooses to take that "one more thing" to the attic or basement, to buy that "one more thing" for the kitchen, dining room, or family room. Each one of us makes the choice whether to say "yes" or "no" to that one more task, committee, obligation, or request. When all that clutter closes in, it's no wonder we become frustrated and emotionally drained. Clutter can be prolific and often doesn't want to go away. We can be so good at putting clutter up or down, but not out. Where is the way out?

My morning started with the sun spraying around the shades and the sounds of spring breaking the silence of the bedroom. I lay there enjoying the new day. The calmness of that morning allowed me to empty my mind of all that lay ahead in the busyness of the next twelve hours. A good night's sleep had put to bed not only the body but the chaos of the mind. I was reminded of Jesus' words from the Sermon on the Mount: "Blessed are the poor in spirit, for theirs is the kingdom of heaven" (Matthew 5:3). I have come to believe that in those words lies the secret to the way out from under the clutter that can consume a life.

How can we feel blessed if we are poor? No one wants to be poor. No one wishes to be always wanting or needing something else before we can live comfortably. No one. Jesus' words seemingly turn our world upside down, but he also shows us the way out. Clutter is powerful, but the words of Scripture are more powerful. With those words Jesus painted a picture of a spiritual life—a spiritual life that has authority over clutter. It is a painting of relationship, a relationship with God. A God who paints, not by rules, but by intimacy. We are called to live each day with God's help, to create a painting not drawn from our performance, but dependent upon the colors and hues of a loving God who wants to be the chief artist in our lives.

"Blessed are the poor in spirit, for theirs is the kingdom of heaven." The poverty Jesus speaks of here is a poverty of spirit. A poverty of spirit so that we recognize our true need and become absolutely dependent on God. To empty ourselves so that God reigns solely in our hearts and minds. I worked on this "emptying" while lying in bed that morning. It's not an easy thing to do, because I had to let go of power and control and invite in the acknowledgement of absolute need, an absolute need for God in my life. Would I put the clutter out, if even for a moment or two, so that I could sense God working in and through me? This spiritual emptying is the antidote to clutter.

The phone rings. Dinner is boiling over on the stove. Papers are everywhere. The family hovers about, and, still, there were things you promised yourself you would get done this day or that you "had to" get done this day. Where is the deliverance from the clutter of our lives? Only as we empty ourselves of those things that clutter our lives and keep us at a distance from God do we receive His true blessings. We are promised the kingdom of heaven. Could it be there, as we make a trip to the swap shop, the dump, or Goodwill? It is not the way up or down, but the way out. Days begin by our choosing a color. May it be the color of God filling your emptiness with all that is His.

TWENTY-SIX

The Poster

"He has been raised from the dead."
Matthew 28:7

What do you remember? How do you remember? By the visuals? By the word or two spoken? Many of the things I remember from my early childhood are flashes of life racing through my memory. There one moment and gone the next. That doesn't make them any less powerful. Just the fact that a seemingly obscure incident is remembered suggests the power of that moment to me. I believe we are all affected by the dynamics of a moment. How unfortunate it is that a negative moment in one's life carries so much weight. It can take ten or even a hundred positive moments to wipe out a single negative one lodged in your memory, and even then the sting of the negative has the power to continue in your life. So, what about all those little positives? Hopefully, they stick with you, and, in that remembrance, something positive will result. This next reflection centers on such a simple incident in my life.

Poster board has been a staple forever in the homes of families with school-age children. I sometimes wonder how many pieces of poster board I have purchased while raising four children—surely a significant investment. The poster board that comes to mind is white. This piece of white poster board was given to each of us in Sunday school during the season of Lent. It would be the key to helping us remember the biblical events of the week leading up to

Easter Sunday. I am a visual learner and so that was a fun activity for me. And, as it turned out, very helpful in my faith journey.

We divided the poster board into frames. We were asked to draw something in each of the frames that pertained to a day and event in Jesus' life the week before Easter. The images didn't have to be sophisticated or numerous, but they were to represent the importance of each day of Holy Week. Palm branches filled the first frame for Palm Sunday and Jesus' grand entrance into Jerusalem. On Monday of that week, in the second frame, I drew a crude table and coins thrown into the air. It was on that day Jesus entered the temple and angrily threw the money changers out, accusing them of defiling his Father's house. Thursday's picture was of a loaf of bread and a chalice, representing Jesus sitting with his disciples at the Last Supper. Friday displayed the cross. Saturday, my rendering of the tomb with a large boulder in front of it. The sadness of this day was conveyed with the images drawn in black with a heavy hand. I don't remember my images for Tuesday and Wednesday, but the image of Easter Sunday is clear. In Sunday's frame the boulder was rolled aside, and near it I drew an angel with rays of light from the sun. That frame was filled with bright color. That piece of poster board has flashed across my mind now for five decades. I've asked myself, *what does this all mean? Why does that poster board remain etched in my memory?*

What I have come to realize is that the events depicted on that poster board in a childhood fashion have come to be hugely important in my life. I've further come to understand the importance and meaning of those events in so many other lives. Those simple images represent a life-giving force in this world, a world that needs all the hope it can muster. From the coins of Monday and the cross of Friday, to the celebratory colors of Sunday, Jesus lives within my life. It was as if in that particular year of my life, in that particular class, with that particular poster board, I allowed Jesus and his life to take up residence in my mind. Through the years those images have grown in my heart, and I have come to realize and affirm more fully the power of Easter week.

When those images flash across my mind's eye, four particular emotions stir within me. Two of those emotions would be expected; the others may be a bit unusual. As those images touch my memory, may I be bold enough to say that today I can more fully appreciate what Jesus felt. Or expressed in another way, it is as if I can realize what it means to be human with all the emotions I believe God feels for and in us. God sent His Son to dwell among us so that Jesus might know our joys and our pains. As we experience life, so Jesus experienced life. I can relate to Jesus in all his humanity but ultimately, too, what Jesus did for me and for you and our world. As I recall my drawings, Monday, Thursday, Friday, and Sunday flash most vividly within my heart.

Have you ever been angry? A silly question. Of course, all of us have been angered by something or somebody. We know what anger is: *how dare that person cut me off in all this traffic? You spilt the milk all over the rug; what a mess! Who drove over my new lawn? I can't believe she left me standing here by myself without even a phone call of explanation! The bank did what? I'm sorry; borrowing my new sweater breaks all the rules. I want it back, now!* Anger is a real emotion for us humans.

As I see my drawing of coins and a table, I can feel anger. I believe what I am feeling is the anger Jesus must have felt: "Then Jesus entered the temple and drove out all who were selling and buying in the temple, and he overturned the tables of the money changers and the seats of those who sold doves. He said to them, 'It is written, "My house shall be called a house of prayer"; but you are making it a den of robbers' " (Matthew 21:12–13). The poster board image stirs the feeling of Jesus' anger. An anger over a material world not getting it right, not getting his message. As I reflect on the image further, I have a deeper sense of Jesus' humanity and the pain he saw in our worldly humanity that separates us from a relationship with God.

Thursday's images of the bread and cup turn my emotion to love. I hadn't seen Da Vinci's painting of the Last Supper when I made those drawings back in Sunday school, but the painting now is a vivid image in my mind: Jesus sitting around a table with his disciples sharing the Passover meal. I have sat around a table with family or friends and shared a meal and known real joy and love in that time together.

It was a warm summer night in the early 1990s—a perfect night to sit outside for dinner and enjoy the cool of the evening. We had served ourselves in the kitchen, and everyone brought a full plate of food out to the table on the terrace. What a treat it was to have the family at home together. The conversation started slowly, but soon became quite animated as everyone tried to get a word in edgewise. Stories came alive as my kids told the tales of their day from summer jobs and camp. Sometimes I wondered if anyone was listening to anyone else, because we all were talking at once. The joy in the sharing was blatantly obvious. There were moments when a story was so funny that we all broke out into belly laughs. This is the laugh that leaves you breathless and brings tears to your eyes. The joy in you explodes forth. But as we sat together at one table, sharing a meal, what I felt most strongly was love. In this I feel richly blessed.

The breaking of the bread and sharing of the cup is a sacred sacrament in Christian churches around the world. In this act we come to know our Lord more fully. "While they were eating, he took a loaf of bread, and after blessing it he broke it, gave it to them, and said, 'Take; this is my body.' Then he took a cup, and after giving thanks he gave it to them, and all of them drank from it. He said to them, 'This is my blood of the covenant, which is poured out for many' " (Mark 14:22–24). Jesus has invited us to join him at the table. Have we accepted that invitation? Have we invited Jesus to sit at our tables?

As I continue to ponder that Last Supper, I feel Jesus' love for his disciples, as he said, having taken his place at the table, "I have eagerly desired to eat this Passover with you before I suffer" (Luke 22:15). In the same way, Jesus said, "You did not choose me but I chose you" (John 15:16). Over the last decade and a half I have felt in a stronger way the call to be more fully a disciple. As I reflect on the hand-drawn images on my poster board, I feel more and more as if I have been invited to sit at the table of Jesus Christ and have grown more and more comfortable accepting that invitation. Why? Because of the love I have come to know from Christ. A love so strong that he was willing to endure the events of Good Friday.

And so now I see the cross on my poster board. That cross created by my hand remains clear in my mind, simply two lines drawn with a brown crayon. The dark brown color made the cross jump out at you. There it was in the fifth frame, standing all by itself. Those two crossed lines have taken on great power for me over the last three decades. They symbolize suffering and forgiveness, sacrifice and redemption.

My two brown crossed lines give me pause to reflect on some of the suffering I have witnessed. A friend who died a number of years ago comes to mind. We met when we served together on a church committee. In that mystical way of friendship, we seemed to "click" from the very start. She was warm, insightful, and a joy to be around. We became close. And so I grew very heavyhearted when I learned she had cancer. At first the diagnosis seemed unreal. And we've all had this next thought: *how could someone so nice and so good be struck with cancer? It just did not seem fair.* She was determined to fight it, but that didn't surprise me. She loved life and wanted to live it to the fullest as long as she could. When she began the radiation and chemotherapy, the aggressive therapy was not easy for her. I wept inwardly when she lost her hair, as I did when I learned how sick she felt. My friend was truly suffering. This realization hit my heart; it was so hard to watch. When she had to be hospitalized because the drug therapy and the cancer began to take control of her body, I moved into a state of real sadness. How could this be happening?

One visit to her in the hospital weighs heavy on my heart. She was sitting up in bed with full coordination of her limbs, but she was not there. She didn't really know me when I first arrived. How sad I felt as we tried to have a conversation. Nothing seemed to make much sense. I didn't stay long, because I could sense the difficulty she had communicating. I left with a heavy heart, grieving the suffering we have to endure. I experienced firsthand how cancer is an unmerciful illness. I experienced the true suffering of a good friend. Suffering is hard. Suffering no matter what its cause is very hard. My friend's life and spirit remain with me; I give thanks for the time we had together, but so too, her suffering has remained in my heart. How horrendous Jesus' suffering must have been that Friday on the cross.

In the final frame of my white poster board is the crudely drawn angel with bright colors surrounding her.

> Mary Magdalene and the other Mary went to see the tomb. And suddenly there was a great earthquake; for an angel of the Lord descending from heaven, came and rolled back the stone and sat on it. His appearance was like lightning, and his clothes white as snow . . . the angel said to the women, "Do not be afraid; I know that you are looking for Jesus who was crucified. He is not here . . . He has been raised from the dead, and indeed he is going ahead of you to Galilee." (Matthew 28:1–3, 5–7)

Heart and Soul

Though the Scriptures say the angel was masculine, my drawing was the classic child's rendering of the beautiful angel with long blonde hair, fairy wings, and a golden halo. The bright colors surrounding her are not scripturally based, but for me they represented what Easter was about—joy. Since that time I have added hope. My faith journey has brought me from my childish joy of Easter to the hope I know in Easter. At first this hope was a thought of the mind and understanding; it is now a feeling of the heart. The places I have been on Easter morning are one of the reasons the joy and hope of Easter reside more fully now in my heart and soul.

Have you been to an Easter sunrise worship service? There is something glorious about the first dawn's light coupled with song and the message of the risen Christ. I have stood by a lake with friends and people of differing churches and different faith journeys and listened while a woman reenacted Mary arriving to find the empty tomb. Wondrously, she brought the scene to life. I have stood with my congregation at a local pond and watched the sun rise over the trees. We sang and listened to a trumpet announcing the risen Christ, with geese honking loudly the coming of the new day and their mating ritual bespeaking new life. I have had the privilege of being in the Rocky Mountains riding to the top of a mountain on an Easter Sunday as the sun rose. The darkened sky began to lighten. The snow reflected that light and sparkled in the newness of the day. The mountain peaks were at their most majestic. The grandeur of the moment overwhelmed me. And I have stood on a beach with the stars fading above. At first, it was so dark you needed a flashlight to read by. But only at first, because the promise of the new day was soon upon us. The sky lightened as the sun broke the horizon, and the trees of the island were silhouetted against the sky, which was turning gentle hues of orange and red. There was something sacred and holy about the birth of the new day, most particularly so because it was Easter.

Each of those mornings has been cold or damp, cool or warm. But the angel announcing Jesus' resurrection was always there. I didn't know the colors of the mountains, or the lake, or the beach when I drew my depiction of Easter Sunday on the poster board. Yet I guess in my heart of hearts I knew that such Easter days existed, because in the birth of Easter morning lay our greatest promise of hope fulfilled. That last frame on my poster board has become so powerful for me. And I have been blessed to witness that power in other people as their faith journeys have matured.

From coins to angels, my drawings of Sunday school on the poster board recall for me and remind me of my journey to a better understanding of Easter. I feel my greatest gift is that this Easter week has moved from understanding to faith. To a faith in the risen Christ who through his ministry, suffering, and death brings me hope. Faith and hope now walk more closely hand in hand. May it be so with you.

TWENTY-SEVEN

Identity

"Destined us for adoption as his children"
Ephesians 1:5

As I walked down the upstairs hall in my home, I passed Christina's bedroom and glanced in. A foot or so beyond the doorway, I stopped and turned back. I stood looking into the room. It was almost bare. Where were the clothes all over the floor? Where were the books, papers, and pens on the desk? Where was all that stuff that was always on the dresser? The light was gone from the nightstand. The closet door was open, revealing few clothes. The space's emptiness overwhelmed me with sadness. Sunlight streamed through the windows, but the room seemed dim because the person who had lived in it was gone. For the first time since my family had moved into our Dover house, Christina's room was not filled to the brim with her things. My heart was heavy. I felt tears in my eyes. Then I thought, *What a strange feeling. I should be standing here in joy, not emptiness.*

Having turned fifteen the prior spring, Christina had decided to go away to school for her last three years of high school. She'd been accepted by a good school. We all were delighted with her success and excited about her new journey. But when she packed up her room and left for the fall term, I felt I'd lost part of my identity. This feeling of loss caused me to search my soul. The last fifteen years ran through my mind like a movie. I reflected on all the things, great and small, that had been central to my life. In my mind and soul, I walked through the days with my children.

At age thirty-three, I'd given birth to my fourth child, Brooks. My life had become even busier than it had been during the previous seven years of motherhood. At that time, no alarm clock was needed in our house. I was an early riser, probably because of all the mornings of getting up to nurse Brooks. His squeaky cries carried through the darkness of early morning into our bedroom. It had become routine for me to be up before the birds. I'd become very good at fumbling around the corner and down the hall to the baby's room without turning on a light. To be kind to my eyes and avoid startling Brooks, I'd turn on a soft, low light. I'd move him from the crib to the changing table for a new diaper. I'd speak softly to Brooks, to settle him down and avoid waking the other children. Sometimes this strategy worked. When it didn't, I'd move quickly to start the feeding process as soon as possible, to cut down the noise level.

I'd settle into the old-fashioned wooden rocking chair in Brooks's room. As he began to nurse, quiet would return. How many hours I spent in that rocking chair, which had belonged to my grandmother! I nursed all four of my children while sitting in that chair. To make it more comfortable and inviting, I padded it with cushions on the back and seat. It was a good, sturdy rocker. How I loved to rock my babies! How I love a rocking chair even today. Now that I have two grandchildren, my rocking has taken on a new wonder. Back and forth. Back and forth. My children loved the rhythmic motion. It soothed both mother and baby. As morning light began to fill the room, my time with Brooks would come to an end. Placing the sleeping baby back into his crib, I'd quietly return to my bed and gently climb in with the hope of getting a few more minutes of rest before everyone was up for the day.

How did the babies grow into toddlers so quickly? Before I realized it, my family was six at the breakfast table in the morning. Breakfast was mandatory in our house. The goal was always to be up early enough and be organized enough that there was time to eat breakfast before going off to school. Bowls of cereal and glasses of orange juice. Bread waiting for toasting. Of course, everyone liked their bread toasted differently. "Yes, you have to finish your juice . . . No, you can't leave the table until you've eaten most of your cereal." The banter back and forth was endless. One by one the children would finish their breakfast. "Upstairs to brush your teeth. No arguing." When all of the children had learned to brush their teeth, I was thankful not to have to go upstairs to do the brushing for them. The breakfast dishes would be piled high by the kitchen sink. I always desperately tried to get them into the dishwasher before I moved to my next activity. If I didn't load them right away, they'd still be sitting there at lunch or even dinner.

The getting dressed for the day's activities was challenging, as was selecting and coordinating the children's outfits. Christina and Elizabeth liked to pick out their outfits, but Jonathan and Brooks gladly let me select theirs. Day after day, I pulled pants over children's legs and shirts over children's heads. How many hours I spent finding two socks that matched! The children's socks often disappeared from their feet even before the children got downstairs. I often wondered where all those socks went.

Somehow, Christina and Elizabeth would be ready on time for the school bus. Because we could see the bus coming up our street, there always was adequate warning for them to grab their coats and bags and get out to the street in time. We made it! The bus stopped right at the end of our driveway. Now, standing in the doorway of Christina's room, I flashed back to standing with her for her first ride on the school bus. We waited with great anticipation. I could feel her excitement. What a big step for both of us! In my mind's eye, I see the photo that I took of her as she climbed the bus's steps for the first time.

With Christina and Elizabeth on the bus, I'd scramble to get Jonathan off to nursery school. Whether Brooks was sleeping or awake, I'd scoop him up, bundle him up, and fasten him into the car seat. My next-door neighbor, Donna, and I carpooled. If it was my day to drive the kids to nursery school, I'd pick up her son first. Some mornings, driving to nursery school was a calm experience; other mornings I thought, *We can't get there soon enough!* Like most of the other mothers dropping off children at nursery school, I'd enter the building with a baby in my arms. Having taken Brooks out of his car seat, I'd carry him down the stairs to the basement nursery school, where I'd drop off Jonathan. Then I'd carry Brooks back up the stairs and put him back into the car seat. Would we make it home in time for his next feeding, or would he fuss the whole way? Always a challenge.

At home a pile of dirty laundry awaited me. Always. The house that we lived in at the time had a wonderful laundry chute off the upstairs hallway, by the bedrooms. The children would simply remove their dirty clothes and toss them into the chute. The chute emptied out right onto the washer and dryer. What a mother's dream! What a brilliant architect. Also, I'd built small bins, painted in bright colors, over the washer and dryer, into which I sorted the clothes. The sorting seemed endless. A load at a time, the washer swished and the dryer hummed. Then folding this and folding that, sorting my children's clothes and placing them in the laundry basket for the trip upstairs. And all those socks that got lost on the children's way from upstairs to downstairs in the morning? Over time the rest of the socks seemed to disappear in the washer or dryer. How could that be? Finally I bought only one type of socks for each child. Then there was half a chance of finding matching pairs!

A visit to the grocery store was usually on the agenda before nursery school let out. When the children were babies, they'd take a morning nap, and then it was off to the store before lunch. Now when I grocery shop, I love seeing babies in the shopping carts. I think about the times when my children were that size. Sometimes they slept through the shopping trip. Other times, I sprinted up and down the aisles, grabbing what I needed while they cried. Of course, they would fall asleep as soon as they were back in the car seat and on the way home.

Over the years, grocery shopping with children always was a challenge, especially when I shopped with all four. The children would ride in the cart, sit on its bottom level, hang off the end. Four children under the age of seven in the grocery store. Somehow, we always seemed to survive. I deserved a merit badge.

My children's favorite lunches were grilled cheese and peanut butter and jelly. Quick and easy. For some mysterious reason Christina got it in her head at any early age that she had invented lunch. As I stood looking into her empty bedroom when she was fifteen, I laughed to myself about this, her greatest invention.

Any of my children who weren't in school all day napped after lunch. As their heads hit the pillow, so did mine. This was the one treat I gave myself each day. If I could nap, the rest of the day was doable.

After nap time, the children took more and more toys from the toy box. "Don't worry about the mess," I told myself. If the children were playing contently, I could do some cleaning. Again, another endless process. Dusting, mopping, vacuuming yards and yards of rug.

As the children got older, I had to find another time slot for cleaning because in the afternoons I had to plan, cook, or act as driver for their Brownie, Scout, and sports activities. The bane of my existence was the boys' Little League baseball. The practices and games always began around five thirty and ran through dinner hour. Jonathan and Brooks would have a snack before baseball. Bill and I had a tag team operation. I'd be out the door to take the boys to Little League as he arrived to take over the home scene of the girls doing their homework. How many early evenings I sat by the baseball diamond! We Little League mothers called ourselves the brigade of folding chairs. Gnats and other insects swirled around; we futilely tried to brush them away.

The girls had their share of afternoon sports, especially field hockey. During the hockey games, their brothers would run around, play on the playground equipment, and whine, "Can we go home now? I'm bored." I'd be on the sidelines cheering. I was where I wanted to be, but still that nagging feeling that there was so much to do hung on. Joy and restlessness resided within me. Time had to be juggled to fit it all in. I asked myself, "Are all these activities necessary?" But the kids loved them, so my answer always was yes. As with any young mother, there often weren't enough hours in the day. By six o'clock the children were tired, and I was exhausted. They also were hungry, so I had to prepare dinner—quickly.

Whenever possible, I bathed the kids before dinner. As I knelt and bent over the tub, my knees and back got a workout. One child in. Scrubbed and out. Next. Scrubbed and out. What a gift it was when Christina and Elizabeth were able to bathe themselves! Then the struggle became, "Are you out of the tub yet?" Many a time I was up and down the stairs numerous times.

But such an early evening was relatively calm. How many times did I end up at the pediatrician's office between four and five p.m.? A stomach ache, a painful ear, a runny nose, a fever—all would strike just when the day was running out of minutes in which to get anything more done. And we always had to wait at the doctor's office. After all, it was late afternoon and the doctor's were behind. A quick diagnosis and we'd head home. Then—again because of the time of day—we'd sit in traffic, inching our way home with commuters. The kids would begin to unravel. I'd try to remain calm behind the wheel, but often I, too, felt my nerves fraying.

Making dinner in fifteen minutes or less became my forte. Fortunately, my children were good eaters. I didn't have to coax them to eat everything on their plate. I enjoyed dinnertime. I liked sitting with my children and talking with them about the day's activities and those scheduled for tomorrow. The sharing was special. To this day I cherish having my family seated around the table. I feel blessed by this incredible gift.

As the day faded, there were still lots of chores to be done. All those toys on the floor of the family room needed to be put away. When I reflect back on all the discussions I had with my children about picking up their things, I grow a bit weak. They were now tired, and I was tired. Yet I wasn't about to spend the rest of the evening in a family room chaotic with toys, so we all would work to clear the floor.

Then one of the children would pick a book to read. Story time signaled that bedtime was near. One by one I'd tuck the children into bed. Then . . . peace.

My children were my life. Their busyness was my life. Our home, with all its chores, was my life. Whenever I spent time away visiting family or friends, returning home felt good and right.

Where did the time go? Standing at the door to Christina's room, I wondered how I used to do it all. How did I do it? It now seemed almost impossible at times. I felt like I lost a little piece of me when Christina left. That was difficult. I pondered, "Who am I now?" My daughter's empty room challenged my sense of self. All the years of childrearing, my identity had been defined by nurturing, cooking, carpooling, doing the laundry, and wiping skinned knees and teary eyes. There were laughter and tears, hard times and joy. Now Christina had left. Yes, I had three more children to love and care for, but the first had left. I no longer would see her every day. In time my other children, too, would make their way into the world, and I no longer would see them every day. Along with a pang of loss, I felt joy. Christina was ready for and excited about her journey ahead. Her independence and growing maturity were to be celebrated. Would she still need me? Of course.

So who am I now? The words of Paul help. God, "destined us for adoption as his children through Jesus Christ, according to the good pleasure of his will" (Ephesians 1:5). Those words from Scripture affirm who I am. I am a child of God through Jesus Christ. Overtaken by a certain humility, I reflect on this my understanding of Scripture. Humility is knowing you are special in your loved one's eyes, but more importantly it is knowing *whose* you are. Humility is the hope that comes from knowing you are God's beloved child. My journey with my children and my faith has led me to understand that I'll always be a mother, just as I'll always be a child of God. Through those two identities I am doubly blessed.

TWENTY-EIGHT

To Kitty

"To those who are good"
Psalm 125:4

My walk took me into the brilliant morning sunshine. Every bird along the way sang praises to the new day. The chirping was welcome company as I set out down the road. As I looked skyward, the freshness of the newly born leaves awakened me to the rebirth of spring and the promises of hope from an eternal God. All this beauty sank into my very being and must have settled most particularly this morning in my heart. But what was it in my heart that was aching to be known and reflected upon during these moments within nature? The name of a friend kept rising to the surface—a nagging "something." As I walked along, I was sure I could feel her in my heart. What did that mean? In my mind I started to explore my relationship with this friend.

I had known Kitty for over fifteen years now. For whatever reason we seemed to gravitate toward each other more as we got to know each other better. We shared a certain respect for each other that I believe brought us closer together. Her expertise in horticulture and extraordinary flower arrangements wowed me. Her admiration of my call to ministry never ceased to amaze me. Kitty carried herself with such grace and poise. She radiated style with humility. We could laugh and joke and ask with genuine interest about each other's lives. She was the type of person I just loved to talk with, because the whole experience made me feel so positive. I recalled some of those conversations and played them over in my mind. They felt good.

Now what does good mean? That's such a generic word. How can I truly do justice to the meaning of this "good" I felt within my heart this morning? As I walked I pondered the thought that good lives within the heart. The heart knows what good means. The heart may not be able to define good, but knows how to respond and react to it. Good has the potential of filling the heart to overflowing. Overflowing with what? Good? But you can't define "good" with good. So I began to explore the goodness I was feeling this morning. What I knew right off was that it had a dynamic that caused me to give thanks as it embraced me.

My step became lighter, and I had this overwhelming desire to try to put into words this mysterious "good" that caused my heart to offer up praise. I use the word *mystery,* because mystery is not explainable but still commands a presence. So what lay around and within this mystery? Perhaps it was the knowledge that I could dip into this well of goodness anytime I needed to by just being around my friend. By rejoicing with her in all her accomplishments. By sharing a story. By sharing a difficult time, knowing we were there to truly listen to each other. By acknowledging our strengths and our shortcomings. By working together. That's what made ours a special friendship.

But sadly, those shared moments came to an end with her untimely death. With the news of her illness, I couldn't believe or did not want to believe that she would soon be taken from me, from all of us who loved her so. But that day came sooner than we all had expected. And then she was gone, and many grieved the loss of a friend, companion, and loved one. Kitty died, and I would never share a laugh with her again, or the opportunity to ask for her advice again, or have an everyday run-of-the-mill conversation with her again.

But was she really dead? Maybe herein begins the understanding of the mystery of the "good" I felt within my heart. As I walked in the beauty of our world that morning, it became clearer that she was not dead to me. Why had I not realized it until then? Maybe I had, maybe I had not, but that morning she was as with me as she ever had been. How did I know that? I knew that because of what I was feeling within my heart. My heart sung with the birds of the good with which I had been blessed through Kitty. Good was our relationship which caused wholeness, a spirit of thanksgiving, and a living beyond the self into the gifts and love of another.

As I climbed a hill, I worked a little harder to exercise my legs. Interestingly, I found I was working my heart a little harder, too. It was beating faster, working to blossom forth even more fully with the spirit of Kitty living within me. Yes, Kitty had passed from this world to a life eternal with God, but she remained with me. That feeling is nothing new to many. As a pastor presiding over a memorial service, I have expressed that sentiment again and again about the departed loved one. "Though departed from us they live on within us always," states my eulogy prayer. I believe that and have witnessed that in my ministry. So what was the mystery of that feeling that morning? As I came down the other side of the hill, I tried hard to put my finger on it.

The mystery is of God. It had to be for me that morning because of the beauty and goodness, warmth and spirit I felt within that mystery. The mystery was resting in my heart, that part of me which is life-giving in so many realms—in the ability to climb a hill, in the ability to love another, in the ability to recapture a spirit and infuse it with life right then and there. I hear the birds and see the new growth. Spring in all its rebirth had propelled me to examine my heart. And there lay Kitty. As I pushed homeward, I rested in our relationship, in all she had been and was, to me and others, the generosity of her expertise and love, and her spirit that remains alive. *How richly blessed I have been,* I thought as I walked up our driveway. *I gave thanks to God for that blessing.*

And a closing prayer came upon my heart: *may God continue to bless all those who mysteriously have within their hearts the love and good of a friend.*

TWENTY-NINE

Ice Cream

"When kindred live together in unity"
Psalm 133:1

I have a confession to make. I am an ice cream addict.

The sign out front read OPEN. The parking lot was full of cars. As one car pulled out, another was waiting to take its place. The three service windows each had a line in front it. I took my place at the third window at the end of the line. As I stood there, I studied the choices of ice cream. There were more than two dozen different flavors from which to choose. Secretly, I was glad the line moved slowly so I had more time to savor my choice. I narrowed the choice down to a select few. This was a serious decision but not just for me; I listened as the group behind me discussed their favorite flavors as well. I was amused by their banter back and forth about the pros and cons of the different flavors. I cleared my head and made up my mind. I waited patiently for my turn. I gave the young girl my order, and she asked, "Is that all?"

I nodded yes, while thinking the whole time, *no, not really, I would love double the amount of ice cream, please, in a bottomless cone.* Fortunately, when the cone was presented to me, it looked big enough to satisfy. I found a seat on a bench and proceeded to lick away.

I watched the people at the ice cream stand with interest. There sat a family of four with the mother eating from a cup, the father licking away at a cone, and two boys flinging themselves around the bench, licking madly as they tried to control the dripping ice cream. Four young girls with cones giggled and laughed in a conversation that only girls their age could enjoy. A distinguished-looking elderly couple sat on the next bench. They each had a cone and were licking carefully so as not to miss a single drip. Their technique was admirable. A family with a young girl sat at a table. I don't know what happened, but the little girl was screaming and the mother was trying to console her. I wondered if another family member had taken her ice cream away. If that was the case, and I had been that girl, tears would most certainly have been my reaction. Ice cream is ice cream, and nobody, but nobody, takes away my ice cream. And then there were the four little old ladies sitting in their car licking their ice cream cones. I couldn't help but think how adorable they looked. They were intent on what they were doing, concentrating hard on not losing a single drip. They sat; they licked.

I was intrigued by the different styles of ice cream cone eating. I hadn't really thought about it, but with so many people parading by with ice cream this evening, I began studying the techniques. There is the lick around the ice cream while turning the cone in a circular motion—tongue extended to maximize the area covered. Some used the "lick up" method, from the top of the cone to the top of the scoop. And then there was the biting style; this works best for ice cream with chunks in it. You bite off that large chocolate morsel, taking just enough ice cream to balance the tastes. Some people were dainty. Some were quick. Some were intentional. Others seemed to savor every lick. Some devoured the ice cream as if there was no tomorrow or someone meant to snatch it away from them.

The people who had chosen their ice cream in cups had their own techniques as well. Some took small bites. Some took whopping spoonfuls. And then there's the technique of turning the spoon over in the mouth and slowly pulling the ice cream off onto the tongue. That's one of my favorite techniques. But I confess, the only true way to eat ice cream if you don't have it in a cone or cup is to eat it right out of the carton with a long-handled spoon. Is there any other way? This is extremely dangerous, though, because before I know it, I can consume a great deal of ice cream from the carton.

I have a priceless Garfield the cat cartoon stuck on my freezer. It is yellowed with age. In the first frame Garfield is studying the carton of ice cream and asking himself, "One scoop or two?" In the next frame he is madly scooping ice cream from the carton into his bowl. In the last frame you see his bowl piled high with ice cream, and he's looking into the carton saying, "I'll leave one scoop." Ahh, but to eat all but one scoop of ice cream out of a full carton. My children kid me that I've been known to eat most of a gallon carton of ice cream in one sitting. I don't think that's entirely accurate—maybe just half a gallon.

As I watched ice cream bringing all those people together, I reflected that there is something theological about ice cream. Or perhaps, better said, there is something mystically spiritual about eating ice cream. Ice cream has the power to bring people of all ages together. On a hot summer night people of all shapes, sizes, and ages come together to feast at the same table of ice cream. Just as each flavor has a different taste and texture, so we have been created with different tastes and qualities. And yet it is the sharing of a common love of ice cream that unites us.

"How very good and pleasant it is when kindred live together in unity!" (Psalm 133:1) wrote the psalmist. In Jesus' prayer before the events leading up to his crucifixion, he prays that we might all be one through him: "The glory that you have given me I have given them, so that they may be one, as we are one" (John 17:22). St. Paul writes to the Corinthian church: "For just as the body is one and has many members, and all members of the body, though many, are one body, so it is with Christ" (1 Corinthians 12:12). I think it is not by coincidence that St. Paul then goes on in the next chapter of his letter to write about the many and varied characteristics of love. The Scriptures again and again call for oneness and unity among us.

Ice cream has the power to unite us. Chocolate sits on top of vanilla and chocolate chip cookie dough on top of black raspberry. An elderly couple licks their cones while a little one, not able to eat fast enough, finds the ice cream running down her fingers. In their own ways both the young and elderly enjoy this creamy cold treat. Ice cream bridges the generations and magically brings us together in a common love.

This feels very spiritual to me. Ice cream has the power to draw us down a common path. To bring the elderly, the teenager, the young adult, middle-aged, and children together. Whether you are sitting in an SUV, an old Ford, or on a motorcycle, dripping ice cream bridges the gap of the generations toward a unity. Christ calls us to a unity of faith and a unity of being. In faith I believe that through this unity our eyes are opened to see the many attributes we can love and respect in others. Unity brings us closer to neighbor and God. My spiritual journey tells me God's hand is at work through ice cream. The mystery of ice cream unfolds one cone at a time through the hand that holds it on a warm summer's night.

IV

Birth and Rebirth

THIRTY

To Birth

"Breathed into his nostrils the breath of life"
Genesis 2:7

At 9:33 p.m. a new baby came into the world. The miracle of life.

Would I ever see my feet again? This was the great question when I reached the eighth month of my first pregnancy. The new life within me swelled. The excitement of the positive pregnancy test had faded with the passing months.

At that time, home pregnancy tests were not available. Rather, the testing was done through blood work at a hospital. As my blood was drawn that first time, I found myself curiously nervous. Would I be pregnant? I certainly hoped so. As I drove home that morning, I wondered how long I would have to wait for the hospital to call. The day dragged on with no call, and I grew increasingly anxious. I remember pacing around our backyard, looking at the life in nature all around me. Was there truly life within me? It was later in the afternoon when the phone rang and the nurse shared the good news. Yes, I was pregnant. And so the life of my first child had begun.

Life took on a new meaning in that moment. Now I had not only my own life to care for, but the life of my unborn child. My elation was colored only by the fact that we had decided not to tell anyone about the baby until the third month of pregnancy. Fortunately, those three months seemed to fly by. I enjoyed telling people I was pregnant with our first child. It felt like the news of the century, worth shouting from the housetops.

In those first months, I also wanted to announce I was pregnant by looking pregnant. All I felt though, was that I was fat. I continued to teach. The students thought it was "cool" that I was going to have a baby. Because I was working, the days seemed to pass faster. My energy level remained high and so I was able to keep up. On one occasion, I could see one of the girls studying me and my stomach. To know her thoughts would have been priceless. My pants became harder and harder to button. Reluctantly, yet with excitement and joy, I gave in to maternity pants.

At long last I was "big enough" to start wearing all maternity clothes. This was exciting. A whole new wardrobe for the "fat" lady. That first trip to the maternity store opened up a new world to me. With those clothes I would be a different person. In fact, I would be seen as two beings. I came to enjoy the looks I got from the outside world. It was as if I finally had the opportunity to share a miracle with all those around me. As I bought my first maternity clothes, my pregnancy felt more real. There was this little life growing in me.

I believe there is something quite wonderful about a pregnant woman. She carries a certain glow; an inner radiance shows forth. That must be part of the miracle—that you can hardly move about, yet still glow. I liked the new me and enjoyed all those months of pregnancy not just for the first but for all four of the babies I carried. Life took on a specialness I had not known before.

What does new life feel like? I often felt it when the baby's elbow or foot nudged me from the inside, as I sat gazing at the sunrise signaling a new day, or in the restful evenings when the stillness allowed for reflection and thanksgiving. There is wonder and excitement as the baby moves within.

What is it about touching the belly of a pregnant woman? Seems like everyone wants to reach out and touch this roundness. Perhaps it is the mystery of life felt but not seen, or the blessing of birth and new beginnings. Perhaps it is the miracle of mother and child as one.

During the middle trimester of my pregnancy, my husband and I traveled south for a vacation, knowing it may be the last time for a long while that we had each other to ourselves. I borrowed a bathing suit and off we went. Looking in the mirror the first time in that bathing suit was a revelation; I really looked pregnant. When I hit the beach, there was no doubt. I loved those beach days, because it was probably the only time I have felt really good in a bathing suit. I had no pretense that I might sport a beautiful figure. Baby and I sunned together to my delight.

The monthly visits to the obstetrician's became routine. Yet when I reflect back on them, they really weren't, because with each visit a new life took shape in ways I hadn't anticipated. How can you describe the first time you hear your baby's heartbeat? It was somewhat surreal, but a blessing beyond words. Those little beats represented life, a life beyond my own. And then came the first ultrasound; we saw our baby for the first time. A martian-type form filled the screen. There was the large head, the body, the arms, the legs, and yes, I could even see the fingers. In one ultrasound, it appeared that the baby was sucking its thumb—so endearing. I had the nurse print out a copy of that one. That one would go in the baby's album. The baby's first picture. Priceless.

But the day I fully realized I carried a life inside me was the day I felt, really felt, our baby kick. Was I suffering from indigestion again or did this little person move within me? It was not very long before I knew that this pushing and poking was from my baby. The times when the baby walked across my ribcage were both a blessing and a curse. Have you ever tried to sleep, or even just get into a comfortable position, when someone is running laps around your belly? I used to put my hand over my swelling belly to feel the movement. This was a comfort in the knowledge that the baby was alive and continually reminding me of the presence of life.

As one of God's clay jars, I submit that we often go about our busy days and take life for granted. Life is all around us, rushing here and there, playing out like a perpetual film. It all seems so very natural and routine. I guess in many ways it is, but is that any reason not to cherish it? When you have a life growing within you life takes on new meaning, or it did for me. This new life was utterly dependent on me. What I ate, how much I exercised, how much I slept and rested all made a difference for this little being growing within.

The prenatal classes we attended stressed care of the self, but it was a curious inborn instinct that seemed to keep me on the right path. I'll be honest—I splurged on ice cream and jellybeans sometimes and enjoyed those times without guilt. But I wanted a healthy baby, and so I took care of myself.

After a round of ice cream, I was more careful about what I ate and the weight I gained. In those last months it would be hard enough to move with any agility without carrying unneeded pounds. And, I wanted to get back into my jeans as soon as possible.

When the crib went up and the bedroom became the "nursery," our home felt complete. In the last weeks before the birth, like many new mothers, I puttered about in the baby's room readying everything for the big day. How many times could I rearrange the baby clothes? I never seemed to tire of it.

A month before my due date, the headmaster of the school where I was working asked for an appointment with me. I prepared all the documents I thought he wanted. When I arrived for the appointment, I found all the teachers and staff waiting to yell "Surprise!" Indeed, I was surprised. I had no idea that they'd plan a baby shower. What fun it was to open all those boxes of cute little clothes and accessories. I was touched by the gesture. As I readied myself for my new life, I was blessed with good friends to walk that journey with me offering their love and excitement.

As my due date approached, the anticipation grew. But we were not ready for the surprise; two weeks before my due date I went into labor. The wait was over, and the work had begun. I was admitted to the hospital in the morning and told it was going to be a while before the baby was born.

The room was painted a hospital green with bed, chair, and machines surrounding me. We settled in for the long haul. The hours passed, and my labor continued without any remarkable headway. I'd been taught in the childbirth classes how to deal with the contractions and was doing so in a fairly successful manner, but the passing hours started to wear thin on me. How much longer would it be? As the afternoon slipped away, life took on a new meaning for me again. Two lives in one: were we to be joined as one forever? How much longer could I sustain this *togetherness?* I was to bring life into this world, but when? If life had ever slowed down, it was in that labor room. Every minute ticked out sixty seconds ever so slowly. I was gaining an everlasting respect for the fact that human life is measured in seconds—moments that make up a lifetime. The question is, what kind of respect do we offer those seconds as we live out each day?

Twelve hours after we passed through the hospital doors, our baby was ready to come into this world. In the end the actual birth was probably no different than most births, except for the fact that it was our baby. This was the life I had been nurturing for nine long months, and this life was ready to breathe its first breath. As I watched the baby emerge into the world, I was crying and smiling all at the same time. This was surely a miracle. To say it was a miracle seems like such a cliché, but it's not really. It has only become a cliché, because we've allowed it to take on that nature. We say to ourselves, life is life and "ho-hum," so what? But as a baby comes into this world, we are reminded of the miracle of birth. The baby cries out and turns pinker and pinker as air fills its tiny lungs. Our daughter began to fling her legs and arms around. As any mother would tell you about her infant, she was the most beautiful baby on earth, not because her features and body were so outstanding, but because this baby was *my* baby. At that moment life is not "ho-hum" but precious and special.

As the nurse laid our daughter in my arms and I looked down at her tiny nose, eyes and mouth, I was elated beyond words. I looked up at my husband, who had stood with me like a trooper through the hours of labor. His smile was warm and tender. We were together as a family. Before I knew it, the nurse whisked our daughter away to the examination table to do all the after-birth testing, while the doctor tended to me. I studied that little life intently as the nurse put her through the tests. She was pink and trying out every muscle in her body. Life is about movement. Life is about using all those muscles, from arms to heart, to stay alive. Without really thinking about it, I reached up to pull the blanket over me, while our daughter lay on the examination table swinging her arms around trying to figure out what had happened and what this world was all about.

In life there is breath, and the miracle of breathing never ceases to amaze me. In those first hours as my daughter lay at my breast, I listened to her breathe. I could hear myself breathing. Breath is life. Breath is a gift from God, because God breathes life into us. I carried my baby within me and nurtured her as she grew, but it is God who has given life. Life is precious; life is fragile. Here was my newborn infant who looked so delicate and fragile. But as I was to learn, babies are more resilient than we think. It's hard work coming into this world. It's a whole new world for them, beginning in those first minutes outside the womb. My daughter demonstrated her resiliency right from the beginning. Fortunately she was strong, because I had much to learn about caring for a baby. As a new world opened up to her, so too, a new world opened up for me. I was now a mother. A role to be treasured throughout my lifetime. This too is a gift from God.

I was blessed with four babies who are now adult children. Each of those births has a story behind it. Each of those pregnancies speaks to the miracle of birth. Our oldest daughter came into this world two weeks early. Our second daughter arrived right on time. With the birth of our first son, a good friend took on the job of babysitting our daughters, and our second son was born after a hair-raising drive to the hospital in a snowstorm. To have life growing inside me was just as special the fourth time as it was the first. With each baby the pregnancy became easier, but never did it lose its thrill, delight, and wonderment. I was coming to appreciate more and more the uniqueness of every life with which God blessed us. My children remind me every day that life is a gift.

THIRTY-ONE

Hospitalization

"Come to me, all you that are weary and are carrying heavy
burdens, and I will give you rest."
Matthew 11:28

Is it possible for time to stand still and at the same time race into an unknown future? Under the right circumstances I believe that happens. It most certainly did for me when a potentially life-threatening health condition took a turn for the worse. In just a moment, the heart condition that I had been managing for over ten years made a sharp turn for the worse without a single warning. Time stood still, and in that sharp turn, raced into an unknown future.

In the cool of an early morning, I had gone to the high school track for my morning run. My plan included speed work to increase my leg turnovers. I hadn't been running long when, uncharacteristically, I found myself short of breath. I pulled back my pace to a jog and took a couple of deep breaths. Not much help. I started to walk and began to breathe deeply. Better, but still not right. My heartbeat was not slowing down, but continued to race much faster than I thought was normal. Walking the next lap of the track did little to slow my pulse. By the second lap, my heart rate had finally returned to normal, and I was no longer aware of it beating. My concern eased. Thinking this was just a fluke, I started back into my workout, but by the time I had run two more laps my heart again started to race. Shortness of breath overtook me, and I was forced to walk. As I walked the next lap, my heart again calmed down, and once more my breathing returned to normal. What was all this about? In all my strenuous exercising over the years I had never experienced anything like this. I was alarmed but not terribly worried, probably because I was so ignorant of what had in fact transpired. When I returned home, I put a call into my cardiologist to report what had happened. The first words out of his mouth were, "You need to come in for a stress test as soon as possible." As I made the appointment, time stood still and raced at the same time into an unknown future.

Dressed for a run on the stress test treadmill, I was anxious to find out what was going on with my heart. Starting at a slow walk everything felt fine. The doctor and technician kept asking me how I felt. Fine, why? As the pace picked up, I began to labor a bit. With the next increase in speed and incline of the treadmill, my heart rate increased dramatically. I didn't feel bad, but more quickly than I would have expected. The doctor ordered the technician to stop the treadmill and end the test. Period. No questions asked.

As I have reflected back on that test over the years, I still hear the alarm in the doctor's voice. I don't know that I was terrified because I didn't yet fully comprehend what had happened, but it was the first time I really began to worry. Without any explicit information, they sent me home and said they'd be in touch after the test results had been fully analyzed. I went home with a giant question mark looming on the horizon.

Later that day the phone call came. The news was not good. Period. What I had suffered at the track and on the treadmill was ventricular tachycardia. The first time I heard the term I said, "Come again?" Simply put, my heart was beating so fast it was life threatening. The exercise had brought this on, but might not be the only contributing factor. There was absolutely no question I needed medication. The cardiologists needed to find the right drug that would control the VTs and not have too many side effects. Electrophysiological testing would be done to determine this. Sitting on the floor leaning up against my bed, I asked, what happens now? Hospitalization. That was a scary thought. Other than at the birth of my children, I had never been hospitalized. What was even scarier was the fact this testing might take up to four weeks. That's a month in the hospital. Unreal. How could I possibly do that? I had four small children at home and a husband who worked full time. In that moment on the phone, I saw my life falling apart. Little did I know at the time how rough it would get.

"So when do I get started?" I would have to wait for a bed in the hospital's specialized cardiac unit. How long would that be? Hard to tell; it could be next week or not for a couple of weeks. The waiting game had begun. Not knowing when I would have to leave home, I began to put my house in order. I wasn't quite sure what that really entailed, but out of pure frustration and fear I started to fix things. I needed to do something that I could control. With that last phone call from the doctor, I felt control slipping away. I needed to do things that I could see physically accomplished something, anything, even if it meant scrubbing the bathroom floor or doing laundry every day so I would leave no pile of chores in my wake. Again time stood still and simultaneously raced into an unknown future.

The phone call came, and I had exactly twenty-four hours of my old life left. By the next morning I was to appear in the admitting office of the hospital. Ready, set, go. I moved like a small cyclone through the house, but instead of tearing the house apart I was putting it back together, wielding all the control I could muster to get the job done. Did I sleep that night? Don't think so. With hugs and many kisses, I left my children. I am sure they didn't fully understand all that was happening and what the weeks ahead held for them. I can still see their faces, and it summons a mixed snapshot of pain and joy. Those little people who made my life so busy and full every day had been stripped away from me for the time being, and yet, by God's grace, it was those faces that gave me strength as I lay in the hospital. The ordeal for all of us had begun.

Paperwork done, I was shown up to my room. I had a bed against the window. All the standard hospital testing, poking, and prodding began. When dinner arrived that first night, I truly wondered how I was going to survive three to four weeks of this. I put the first bite in my mouth. It was absolutely bland. I'm not a picky eater, but this was really tasteless. When the intern came in to check on me, he commented on the fact I had eaten almost nothing. "But it's like colored cardboard," I complained. Apparently, all food served on that floor to cardiac patients came through with the order to be salt-free. I pleaded with the intern to return the salt to my diet. After he checked it out, I was granted the return of salt to my food. Such a small thing, but I reveled in that little bit of control of my life which, from the beginning of this whole episode, was slowly being stripped away from me.

The next morning I was prepped for the first of my procedures. A wire was to be inserted into my heart for the electrophysiological testing. As I rode down the hall on the gurney, I studied the tiles in the ceiling and the people's faces we passed. Everyone seemed to be peering down at me. A feeling of smallness overtook me. I was glad the doctors had started the sedation, because I knew I would have been extremely nervous otherwise. They opened the doors to the surgical room, revealing machines and equipment that were daunting. Voices around me seemed surreal. As they spoke to me I just wanted to say, *forget the pleasantries and let's get on with this—just knock me out.*

I woke up back in my room with a little curl of wire taped to my upper left chest. With this wire now in place the doctors could control the beating of my heart. I had been told that, but had no idea what it would feel like. I was soon to find out.

I had talked with my doctors about the drugs they wanted to test on me. The long, hard-to-pronounce words meant nothing to me. It was explained that I would start taking a drug. We would then wait until it had started to take effect on my heart and body. It was further explained that some of the drugs would act quickly, and others would take a day or two to build up in my system. The same applied to stopping the drugs. Some would leave my system quickly while others would take time. The reason for such a long hospital stay became clearer. I had to be monitored carefully with the administration of each drug, and that could not happen overnight.

I was given the first drug. It was incredibly tedious to sit by and wait for it to build up in my system. But that was just the beginning of endless hours of waiting. How strange it felt to be lying in a hospital bed and feeling so well. But that would change, as I discovered, with the various drugs entering and leaving my system. When the first drug had taken hold after twenty-four hours, a team of doctors and technicians appeared at my door with machines and wires and lots of really frightening stuff. One of those frightening machines was a defibrillator. The "paddles" were wheeled right up next to my bed. I looked them over in disbelief. This device was used to bring people back to life. Was I going to lose my life here in a hospital bed? They must have thought there could be a chance my heart might react in a life-threatening manner as they performed the tests. I got used to looking at that machine with every test, but it was a solemn reminder of the danger of the testing and the seriousness of my heart condition.

There was no sedation involved because the doctors wanted me to have a clear head so I could interact with them. How bad could this be? Not so comfortable, I discovered. It was weird to lie still and feel my heart racing along. *I should be running, not just lying here.* Throughout the procedure the doctors carried on a conversation with a question here and there directed toward me. The testing didn't take long. The machines were disconnected from that little wire hanging out of my chest, and the waiting started again. How long would it take for the drug to work its way out of my body? I don't remember, but as far as I was concerned, it would be too long.

After a week, I had settled into a routine of living in a hospital under those bizarre circumstances. I was given permission to shower, get dressed, and spend the day moving around the hospital floor, if I felt well enough. I had a heart monitor on so I was carefully watched. The monitor hung around my neck on a soft cord. I had some shirts I could wear that had breast pockets, able to hold that little box very nicely. I was determined not to let my muscles atrophy and so I spent a lot of the days walking. The hospital was set up in such a fashion that the inner workings of the building came up through its core, creating a circular hallway. I would walk around and around the core, then turn and go back the other way. It became a game of wind and unwind. The nurses told me how many times I would have to go around in order to walk a mile. To keep my mind occupied I would spend hours counting the number of circuits I had made around the hall. How many miles could I cover in one day?

A rude awakening came when a drug sent me for a loop. I woke up feeling like I was truly going to die. I lay in the fetal position under the covers wanting the world to go away. The cardiologist arrived that morning and didn't even ask how I was doing. It was blatantly obvious this was not the drug for me. He sat on the edge of the bed and began speaking to me with a soft tender tone. I just moaned and curled up tighter. Make it go away, make it go away was all I thought. I desperately needed a human touch, and so I stretched out my leg and touched him with my foot. He said nothing and allowed me to press my foot into him a couple of times. I was such a "basket case." He knew this little action was harmless but necessary to keep me going.

As I lay there feeling as if I was going to die, time stood still, and at the same moment, raced into an unknown future.

It took hours for the drug to begin to wear off. The nurses and interns were wonderful to me. They had seen that reaction before and knew how to care for me. Mercy seems like a far-fetched word to explain what unfolded in those painful hours, but over the years it has come to feel more and more like that: "Blessed are the merciful, for they will receive mercy" (Matthew 5:7). Mercy describes compassion shown by one person to another. Mercy is extended by a person who has the power to punish, but chooses not to. The doctors' intent was clearly not to punish, but as I lay there feeling like death warmed over, it didn't feel like that to me. I was being punished by my body; it had failed me. Thankfully, the doctors chose not to punish me any further by continuing the testing of that particular drug. I have come to recognize mercy in its many different faces. For me, blessed were the nurses as they tended my very broken body and spirit.

Within a day or two of my stay, I had been moved into a private room. There was no way my husband or I would survive this ordeal otherwise. I needed space, and perhaps some control over that space. Ironically, at times that made me feel so alone. It was like a self-imposed imprisonment. As I reflect back, I wonder how I could have felt so alone with nurses, technicians, and doctors surrounding me every day. They were all so kind and understanding. It was the loss of personal contact that hurt. I desperately needed familiar faces and conversations. My visitors became the light in those long, dark days. I would take them on my walk around the floor. We would sit on the bench by the elevators and stare out the window at the city. We would gather in the family waiting room for conversation. On the days when the drugs got the best of me, I would lie in the bed and just let them talk to me. One time a friend arrived to find my broken body and spirit just lying there looking out the window: a view forever etched in my memory. She pulled up a chair close to the bed and just smiled. The blessing in that light was overwhelming. The power of a smile took on a different meaning. What a blessing. I have tried to remember that moment and offer it to those in times of despair, as well as in the everyday encounters in the grocery store or catching someone's eye on a sidewalk. So simple, yet so easily forgotten or taken for granted. Does it really make a difference? Yes.

After more than two weeks of confinement in the hospital, I received a treat. I was allowed to go outside for a bit. It was a bright autumn day; the sun shone brilliant against the blue sky. The nurse and I rode the elevator down to the lobby, got off, and headed for the door. It felt good to be at ground level and out of my "tree perch" some twenty floors up. When the sun hit my face and the fresh air entered my lungs, I couldn't believe how really good that felt. When you are outside every day, you forget what a gift that is. The whirr of air conditioning units was replaced by the hum of traffic. Sitting on the wall just outside the main entrance, I lifted my face to the sun and drank in every ray. I took deep breaths as if for the very first time. The out-of-doors mesmerized me into a peaceful stupor. To be back in civilization: the cars, the people bustling by, the street noise were their own special blessing that day. The moment passed far too quickly before I was returned to the sealed environment of the hospital floor.

A routine developed for my days. This and that, and this and that, helped to keep me sane and occupied. In reflecting back, I believe it was in the moment I truly surrendered to the whole situation that a certain peace came and helped relieve the anxiety and restlessness of body and spirit. There was nothing I could do but play by the rules of the day. I surrendered to the doctors, to the nurses poking and prodding, to the plain meals and often sleepless nights. Why worry about being tired? I wasn't going anywhere or doing anything the next day. Once surrender of the body came, it was easier to surrender to an inner peace of mind and spirit. A certain trust was emerging. I had this condition. It was not going away. It had to be controlled. The doctors and nurses were committed to finding a drug that would give me back some semblance of life as I had known it. Friends and family offered their support and love. My inner being took a different path on its spiritual journey. A journey not entirely recognizable at first, but one that would grow as the days became more challenging the longer the hospital stay.

At the three-week mark the doctors gave me permission to go home for a couple of hours. A ride in a car never felt so good. My home never looked so good. My kids in my arms, away from the hospital, never felt so good. Life at home had been turned upside down with my hospitalization. It was hard on everyone, and I now knew what a blessing my husband had been in holding everything together for that month. And for that I give thanks. Returning to the hospital was extremely difficult.

The process was endless. The hospitalization was timeless. When would this be over? After more than three weeks, it just had to be soon. It was then that the doctors announced they'd found a drug for me. I could see the exit door. Was it possible? One more test and I was good to go. I traveled over to the doctors' office for the infamous stress test. As this test had condemned me to three weeks of hospitalization, so it would set me free.

I felt good as the test began. With an increase in speed and incline I broke into a moderate run. And then. And then, in a moment I will never forget, my heart started to race and the doctors ordered the test stopped and pulled me off the treadmill. My heart stopped racing, but I died a million deaths. The drug had failed. I had failed. The endlessness grabbed me in a relentless hold, and my spirit completely collapsed. By the time I was returned to my hospital bed, I had dissolved in tears. I curled up in the bed and wished the world away. No. No! My family, too, was devastated by the news. How were they going to survive this ordeal much longer? Nerves had worn thin and patience was elusive. Time stood still and simultaneously raced into an unknown future.

I was afraid. Was I ever going to get my life back again? Fear swallowed me up, and I seemed to go down for the last time. There seemed to be no breath left in me. No words to console me. No future ahead of me, short of that hospital bed. The doctors tried to assure me they had another good drug that they would administer, let it build up in my system, and then retest me. How long? How long would that take? Another week. Those words rang in my ears like a sentence to hell. A hell of endless hospitalization, loss of control, life without my husband and children, broken spirit. How could I do that? How could I do that one more day, let alone one more week? The answer? I had to. I had to have the strength and faith to dig deep, deeper than I had ever dug, to persevere. I had to do it for myself, but more importantly, for my family. I rolled over in the bed and began the drying-out phase.

As the morning slid into afternoon and then merged into darkness, I resigned myself to the time frame of one more week. It was in the next couple of days that I discovered a new path for my spiritual journey: "Come to me, all you that are weary and are carrying heavy burdens, and I will give you rest" (Matthew 11:28). It wasn't the surrendering to the ordeal of hospitalization that gave me rest, but it was in the giving over to the Lord of all that I was carrying. Mustering up all the faith I had, I turned away from control to trust that the Lord would be there to help me carry that last burden. When that finally settled into my heart, the final days were not as hard as I thought they might be. That type of surrender by giving *over* instead of giving *up* freed me to walk the path before me with more courage. The "rest" Christ gave was not in a bed, but of the heart and spirit. There was no doubt this next week was going to be difficult, but with faith it would be doable.

Would I ever get my old life back? Thankfully, no. For throughout the whole month and all the trials of hospitalization with a life-threatening illness, I was transformed. As I reflect on it, I was changed in a way that bespeaks a mystery shrouded in faith. I could say that in the end I found God. Yet I don't know if that's entirely accurate, because God was not to be found, but embraced. God was never lost to me. It was our relationship that had been clouded over by the issues of health and the world of medicine. It was as my faith grew that I came to embrace more and more my relationship with God through Jesus Christ. My faith became my strength. My faith kept me walking down the path of a spiritual journey that has led to a whole new level of relationship and revelation. Is it possible for time to stand still and simultaneously race into an unknown future? For me, time may stand still in the moment of trial, but it no longer races to an unknown future, but to a future that opens wide to light and the arms of a loving, caring God. As I have come to love and embrace God more and more on my journey of life, I have found the old cast away and in Christ a new creation. It is with thanksgiving for each new day that I embrace this new creation of me.

By the end of the week I had passed the stress test and left the hospital with a lifesaving drug. Nine years later I ran the Boston Marathon.

THIRTY-TWO

Expectation

"New wine into fresh wineskins"
Mark 2:22

When realization meets expectations, the heart and mind pause and think.

A lifetime is filled with expectations, and many of those expectations have a strong history, from the past and stretching into the future. Where does the expectation/realization cycle begin? As we mature, we master skills that bring us significant satisfaction and expectations as well. Those skills are of the mind and body. A formal education builds the mind, and with it, the skill to learn and master even more complex facts and information. Worlds open up as our knowledge expands. Through the process and with the successes in learning, I began to set expectations for myself. Such was also true of the physical body. I ran "like the wind" when I was only in kindergarten. I made many first-string athletic teams. As I reflect, I see I was gifted with an ability that led to success upon success in the sports world. The expectation that I could play the athletic game well or even exceptionally expanded with age. I put a lot of pressure on myself. If I was going to play the game, I was going to play it to my full potential, and the expectation was that I would do well. I would succeed, win, or any other label you might place on it.

I continually set expectations for myself, but I was also very aware that others were building expectations of me as well. When I played the games of life well, the expectations fed my soul to reach a higher success. When the games of life eluded me, the expectations weighed heavy on my heart and dragged me down.

One beautiful day not long ago, a certain realization crashed headlong into expectation. My heart seemed to sink with the realization that maybe I could no longer play the game the way I had in the past. A certain aloneness fell upon me. All that strength that I had had year after year, season after season, seemed to be drying up. The harder I tested my physical body, the less strength I could achieve. All that strength seemed for naught. Memories of the Boston Marathon faded.

I realized in that moment I could no longer live up to the expectations set for me—not only by others, but by myself. It occurred to me that I really didn't want to live up to those expectations. I felt tired, weary of body, mind, and spirit. I was weary of always being expected to hit a good shot, run a certain distance at a certain speed, or lift more weights. I was weary of always being expected to remember "this about that" and "that about this." I needed someone or something to lift my spirits so I would not always have to be the "cheerleader" in life.

As this realization about expectations struck me, I began to wonder what was next. *What will I do with this realization? I think I will have to live with it for a while.*

Questions began to spring up in my head and heart. Was there too much outer strength and not enough inner strength? I have always loved anything athletic. Was it time now to tone down the outer achievements and reach within? Was it time to relax the expectations of myself with the hope that as I did, others might follow suit? How hard would it be to lighten up and not try so hard? How difficult would it be to enjoy life from a different vantage point? Could I be happy standing in that new place?

What is it that expectations do to us? Are they life-building or life-threatening? Is there an expectation that is paramount? How do I weigh what is truly important in life? I'm sure there are no right or wrong answers here. But that doesn't make the contemplation of this issue less valuable. Perhaps it even makes it more valuable. What it boils down to is the *self*. Who is your *self*? Do we really know who our *selves* are? Do these selves drive expectations and realizations? Does there come a time to embrace an acceptance that we might not have preferred? Was it now time for me to embrace the acceptance of who I was and who I am now? With reflection, though I have grown and changed, still I believe I am who I was created to be. Is it time now to have a love of self, world, and God from a different vantage point?

In the gospel of Mark we read a parable that speaks about new life: "And no one puts new wine into old wineskins; otherwise, the wine will burst the skins, and the wine is lost, and so are the skins; but one puts new wine into fresh wineskins" (Mark 2:22).

Is it time to put new wine into fresh wineskins? Is it time for me to put on a new self? Is it time to accept this new self does fit and will serve me well, and that the new self is not the old self? As my realization meets expectations, I have faith that God will provide as changes in my life continue to unfold. In my acceptance of a new self I see new possibilities unfolding. I feel a new comfort and challenge in my life and spiritual journey. I feel transformed. In all this I offer up praises and give thanks for this new realization.

THIRTY-THREE

To Die

"Those who believe in me, even though they die, will live."
John 11:25–26

The phone call came in the middle of the afternoon. It was Nancy, the nursing home coordinator. One of my favorite elderly ladies had been taken to the hospital, and the prognosis was not good. She was weak and every breath was a struggle. Would I have time to come and see her as soon as possible? Of course. As I drove over to the hospital, I contemplated what I was going to find when I got there. Would she know me? Would she even be awake? Would she be lying there in the bed sleeping?

I made my way to my friend's room and found Nancy sitting by her bedside. The room was quiet and peaceful; even the noise of the hall didn't make it around the corner and into her room. I acknowledged Nancy and asked her to fill me in on the details. She told me about the events leading up to my friend's admission to the hospital. The prognosis didn't sound hopeful. The nurses and doctors at that point were only keeping my elderly friend comfortable. Death was at the door. It was only a matter of time now. Nancy and I sat quietly at her bedside. A word here and there was exchanged between the two of us.

As we listened to my friend's soft breaths moving in and out, we commented on how comfortable she appeared. We offered a word or two about our experiences with her. We sat in silence. Nancy commented on how lovely she looked and what a beautiful person she had been both physically and personally. We sat in silence. I asked if her family had been notified and was told they were on the way. We sat in silence. A nurse entered and broke into our thoughts as she checked our friend's vital signs. They were weak. We sat in silence. "What time is it?" Nancy asked. That really didn't matter, but gave us an excuse to relate to one another. We sat in silence.

Nancy and I don't know how long we sat at our elderly friend's bedside. We were looking at her face and watching the ever-so-slight movements. And then the movement stopped. The next breath did not come, and the breath after that did not come. Nancy and I turned to face each other. We were sitting very close. We said almost in unison, "She has died."

We sat in silence for another moment. I turned to Nancy and asked if she wanted me to pray. She nodded and said, "I'd like that."

We sat in a moment of silence before I started to pray. I began with words of comfort that I knew from burial liturgies, but soon found myself not being able to think of what to say next. But through the guiding Spirit, more words came. The words fell from my grieving heart in a whisper. I felt a love and peace surrounding us. We offered an *amen* together, and the room became completely silent once more. And so we sat in silence. We sat for a while longer before the nurse came in and confirmed that our friend had in fact died. We asked that she not cover her, as we wanted to look upon her face for a few more moments. I wanted to say good-bye by looking into her serene face, which I believed opened the window to her departing soul moving to its rest with God. Her earthly life had ended, and her life eternal had begun. The mystery of the truth of God's ever-present, never-ending love surrounded and held me as it took my elderly friend, Hazel, on to the next life.

It was unsettling to feel both sadness and joy in that moment. But I did. How could that be? To feel the emotions at either end of the continuum. I felt a sadness, because my heart was heavy. I felt a joy, because joy is from God. A wonderful woman who had lived a generous and full life was gone from me, her friends, family, and our earthly world. Hazel was now at rest in the eternal existence promised to us by God through Jesus Christ, the Son. Jesus said, "I am the resurrection and the life. Those who believe in me, even though they die, will live, and everyone who lives and believes in me will never die" (John

11:25–26). I believe that. It has been a journey to that belief for me with many ups and downs, but a journey well worth the living.

In death there is great sadness because of the emptiness that overtakes the heart and soul. In death there is great joy, because there is rest, a relationship with God fulfilled, and also the power of hope. In these, there is the greatest and purest of love holding a life precious to those on earth and those above. The Holy reaches down and receives unto itself the greatest of gifts, a life. And then a life at rest in all its fullness settles into the arms of God, our Creator; the Son, our Redeemer; and the Holy Spirit, our Comforter.

Hazel now is at rest. There is a lasting peace that surpasses all our understanding.

THIRTY-FOUR

Faith

"Now faith is the assurance of things hoped for"
Hebrews 11:1

I was driving home late in the evening from a meeting. My thoughts were filled with the discussions of the night. About halfway home it started to rain. I turned on my wipers to see the road more clearly. As I passed through a low spot on the route home, I drove into a fog covering the area. The cool rain was hitting the hot pavement, causing a mist to rise from the road. In spots it swept across the road in great clouds, and in other places, it was a dense bank of white. I turned off my high beams to see the road better. It helped, but I decided to switch on my fog lights as well. The fog engulfed the car, and the trees alongside the road became faded giants. I slowed down and crept along. The turns came upon me quickly, and I negotiated them. The road continued to stretch into the fog. It was eerie. It was mysterious.

Faith is a lot like that. We travel the road of life both in the light of day and the darkness of night. The journey can be easily marked. The path can lead to unknown turns. The road splits, and a decision has to be made. "This way or that way?" On that road, we like to be in the driver's seat, because we are then in control. But it is at those times when the road ahead is not defined that we need something beyond our own control. Do we have the courage to turn outward, away from our own devices? Can we embrace the fog of uncertainty? The fog is like a faith that surrounds and holds us. It makes us slow down and take note of the road, the path, the journey. It is mysterious in that way.

Faith is the cool refreshing rain of God hitting the hot pavement of our life—a pavement that has been heated up by the busyness of a hectic, stressful life. We are hot from all the energy we produce from trying to get it all done, from trying to keep our heads above water, from providing and producing, organizing and scheduling. God sends His cleansing rain upon our journey, causing us to slow down and open our eyes more fully. We turn off the high beams of life and turn on the softer fog lights and allow a faith to guide and lead us along the pathway. This is a faith that mysteriously engulfs us. We move through it and with it, not always knowing what will happen next. It is the mystery of trusting in something we can't put a finger on, control, or see a way through. It is the mystery of faith.

What is it about the mysterious that draws us in? I spent many years trying to understand the mysterious, trying to put a label on it, to put a face on it. I thought if I could only do that, many things could be explained away. A certain level of discomfort in the elusive and unseen plagued me. Through reflection and experience, I have now come to understand that discomfort came from lack of control. I wanted to be in control. I thought that was what was expected of me. If I could control the physical world around me, I should be able to control my faith as well. But, as my spiritual journey matured, faith turned out to be far more mysterious than I realized.

Like most do, I struggled with faith. How do I get it? Where do I look? How will I know when I have it? How do I define faith? The Bible has a clear definition of faith: "Now faith is the assurance of things hoped for, the conviction of things not seen" (Hebrews 11:1). This was a good starting place for my understanding, because in essence I wanted to understand the true meaning of faith. As my spiritual journey has grown and I have grown, I have needed something more. For me there needed to be more than a definition of words. Then came the moment I realized I didn't need to know *about* faith but rather *know* faith experientially. I knew I truly could embrace a faith for all time and experiences. It was trusting in the mystery of an all-surrounding and all-engulfing faith that held my heart. To allow faith to engulf me like a gentle fog. A fog sent by God to cool my soul from the heat of the journey.

THIRTY-FIVE

The Relationship

"I trust in the steadfast love of God forever and ever."
Psalm 52:8

Many special friends have joined me as I have traveled my spiritual journey. Over the years I have been blessed with relationships that have healed and edified me, comforted and brought joy to me. In large ways and small ways each has transformed the path on which I have been journeying. Each has transformed me in some manner. As I draw my reflections to a close, I think of one friend in particular. From her and my revelations about our relationship, I have come to better know my relationship with God. Maybe even glean a better understanding.

Life exudes from every pore of this special friend. Her smile invites you in, and her gentle manner holds you close. Her ears are open, and her heart listens. Conversation flows easily with her, and the topics are as varied as the blossoms of spring. There are the colors of laughter and shades of seriousness. Words of wisdom flow from her experiences. Words of knowledge fall from her tongue, because she is such an avid reader of all kinds of literary works. The hours, days, and years we have spent together have been a gift to me. Why a gift? Because she is always a present to me, and invites me to open myself up to enjoy the gift of relationship.

In all that there is one curious factor. I have often wondered over the years whether she really counts me as a good friend. I know in my heart and in the times together she does, but I still wonder if I am a good enough friend. How can she like me so much when she seems to have so many other friends who seem to be far more important than me? Her other friends appear more interesting and exciting than I perceive myself to be. The times and adventures they share seem more intriguing and more fun than what we do together. Does our time together feed her as much as when she travels in the circles of her other friends?

We set a date, and I have even wondered whether she would show up. Not having faith in myself, I figure chances are good she will call at the last minute and say circumstances have come up and she won't be able to make it. I feel the disappointment before it happens. But rarely, very rarely, if ever has she stood me up. I know inside that she is not built that way, that she would never do that to me, but my inner self still questions my worth as a friend. She has all those more exciting friends; why spend time with me? *Maybe because you are a special friend, Ingrid,* I quietly and carefully whisper to myself. I hope and pray so.

With reflection I have drawn a comparison between the relationship I have with that friend and my relationship with God. That reflection has helped me to better understand God and solidify my relationship with Him. And so I began to line the questions up. With all the other truly exciting people in this world, why would God want to be my friend? With so many people to "play" with who are probably far better playmates than I, why would God want to be my friend? With so many relationships to be cultivated and embraced, why would God want to know me personally? With so many more exciting adventures to enjoy with other people, why would God want to be my friend? With so many other needs and people to be healed, why would God want to make me his chosen daughter? And the questions go on in a similar manner.

Why? Because I *am* special in God's eyes. Though I might think it, I know God does not play favorites. Though I feel it at times, God will not choose another soul over me. God is so big and so full of love. God's ears are open to me and to any and every one who comes knocking. The door is always there ready to be opened to the next chapter in life. God will and wants to laugh with me. God will and wants to walk the path of sorrow with me. God listens. God hears. God wants to grow His relationship with me. I have come to embrace more fully the truth that God is there with an open heart ready to have a relationship with me. It is me who stands at the door and needs to turn the doorknob and open myself to God. It is me who needs to want to have that relationship, and then do something to fulfill that want.

Am I worthy to come before God? To come and offer up to Him all that I have been, am, and will be? To have the faith that our relationship is founded on such a great love that I receive forgiveness as I confess? To have the faith and trust that in returning to the stronghold of God's hands and heart I will be embraced with a relationship that carries with it a blessed holiness? Can I understand that relationship with God? Probably not all the time, but that does not mean I will be stood up, that God is too busy for me. That doesn't mean that I don't share a special relationship with God.

When I ponder that relationship and God feels so far off and far too mysterious, I turn to Jesus. The words of an old familiar hymn sing in my heart, "What a friend we have in Jesus . . ." As I trust in my budding and growing friendship with Jesus, a man of earthly and divine nature about whom I can read records of his years on earth, my heart and faith grow stronger. If I have known Jesus the Son, I have known God the Father, the gospel of John promises. Through Jesus, the risen Christ, my hope blossoms forth with the colors of a loving and caring relationship that is at the very foundation of friendship. But still in moments of doubt I ask, why would Jesus, the Christ, choose me as a friend? What is it about me that would cause Jesus to wish to grow a relationship? As with my special friend, I ask *why me?* In reflection I remind myself I am one of God's blessed children, children precious and sacred in the holy eyes keeping watch over me, over us. That's why.

Through the reflections of my life, I've discovered that I have been transformed through relationship and all that I have gleaned from those relationships and the circumstances surrounding them. As I look to the future, my faith in my relationship with God through Jesus Christ grows stronger by each experience and by the minutes, hours, days, and years I have to live. My spiritual journey stretches out before me with God as my true friend, comforter, and savior.

> "But we have this treasure in clay jars,
> so that it may be made clear that this extraordinary power
> belongs to God and does not come from us."
> *2 Corinthians 4:7*

ACKNOWLEDGEMENTS

The writing of my memoir has been a profoundly spiritual journey for me. Along the way I have been touched, encouraged and loved. It is my sincerest wish to acknowledge certain people who have most particularly walked this path with me.

As a mother many weeks, months, and years are spent wiping noses, preparing meals, playing taxi driver, hugging, and offering words of encouragement to your children. What a true gift it was when I turned to my oldest daughter, Christina, one evening and announced to her I was writing a book and her face lit up with excitement. My heartfelt "thank you" goes out to Christina who supported me, critiqued my ideas, listened to my endless babbling and loved me as my manuscript took shape. We walked this journey together for more than nine months as I was writing the first draft, without sharing this project of mine with anyone except my sister. For me it was a certain specialness shared between a mother and a daughter who has grown into an intelligent and gracious woman.

Thank you to my sister, Gretchen, who read the initial manuscript and boldly asked, "What are you going to do now?" When I replied I wasn't sure, she told me to go get a freelance editor and work towards publishing. And so I extend my thanks to Susanne Lakin who took on the job as a freelance editor for my manuscript. She worked patiently and professionally to help me better shape my words, thoughts and stories. I thank her for her time, connection, and caring through the editing process and beyond. As the time came closer for publishing I again turned to my sister for her help and again she put forth some ideas and her valuable personal experience. It was then that I had the wise guidance from Zick Rubin and Morris Rosenthal, who I thank for their time and expertise in their fields. And a thank you to my husband who read the initial draft in amazement and to my son, Jonathan, who read the proof with careful scrutiny.

Putting it all together for publishing, I thank Fred Ariel and Jean Giuggio of Ariel Design for their thoughts and expertise, working patiently and professionally with me to develop my ideas and vision. To see a major part of my personal spiritual journey in black and white for others to share was moving. This path has now come to an end, but in many ways it opened up to me many more paths to venture down. With thanks for all the help I received during this process I look forward to my continuing journey and connections I will make along life's journey in the future.

Ms. Ruth Bushmich
30 Julio Dr
Shrewsbury, MA 01545

- Thank You -

Made in the USA
Lexington, KY
10 February 2010